Spite for Spite

El desdén, con el desdén

Smith and Kraus *Books For Actors*

THE MONOLOGUE SERIES

Spite for Spite

by Agustín Moreto

translated by Dakin Matthews

Great Translations for Actors

SK
A Smith and Kraus Book

A Smith and Kraus Book
Published by Smith and Kraus, Inc.

Copyright © 1995 by Richard Matthews
All rights reserved

Manufactured in the United States of America

Cover and Text Design by Julia Hill

First Edition: December 1995
10 9 8 7 6 5 4 3 2 1

Library of Congress Cataloguing-in-Publication Data

Moreto, Agustín, 1618-1669.
[El desdén, con el desdén. English]
Spite for spite / by Agustín Moreto; translated by Dakin Matthews. --1st ed.
p. cm. -- (Great translations for actors)
Includes bibliographical references.

ISBN 1-57525-002-0
I. Matthews, Dakin. II. Title. III. Series.
PQ6416.D413   1995
862'.3--dc20   95-22918
CIP

for Lillian

Preface

This translation was commissioned by the Old Globe Theatre of San Diego and prepared for a possible production, which as yet has not been staged. (Readings with music were done, both at the Old Globe and during the Taper New Works Festival, by the Antaeus Company.)

The fact that it was—from the beginning—a theatrical, rather than a scholarly endeavor, will explain much about the kind of translation it is and the kind of very practical choices I have had to make in doing it.

What, then, to make of an edition of this text—especially one that looks suspiciously like a critical one—with introduction, bibliography, appendices, and all that apparatus? For whom, exactly, is it intended?

Frankly, I intend it to be "for all markets." Audience members who have seen and heard the play will have a rather thorough record, if they wish one, of what I hope was for them a pleasant experience. The casual reader of play texts will find an accessible and not-too-daunting example of a wonderful seventeenth-century Spanish comedy, a genre he or she may unfortunately be unacquainted with till now. The student will have a literary text dense enough to reward close reading, and thorough enough to suggest further possible areas of research and enjoyment. And the scholar will, I hope, be not too disappointed either with the accuracy of the rendering or the critical information and analyses presented in the apparatus, and will be encouraged to return to the original with enthusiasm and freshness.

But the most important thing is that it is intended for the reader of English. Accordingly, I have tried very hard not to discourage the English reader by leaving untranslated large chunks of critical material in Spanish (or any other language), or by constantly referring to works in foreign languages that the normal English reader would have neither interest in nor access to. Even as I have tried to find English linguistic and literary equivalents in the translation, so in the critical material I have continually referred to similarities between Moreto and, for example, Shakespeare or the Restoration dramatists—not because I think there was any direct influence one way or the other, but only by way of making the unfamiliar somewhat more familiar.

I have many people to thank for their assistance in preparing this version—first and foremost the wonderful actress, director, translator, and playwright Lillian Garrett-Groag, who first put me on the track of this play, who watched over me through the whole process, who kept a critical eye on my Spanish, who proofread the whole thing, and to whom the final product is dedicated. If faults remain, they are entirely mine, and I can only say there would have been many, many more without her sharp eye and soft heart.

Thanks also to Mark Hofflund of the Old Globe, who encouraged me from beginning to end and was my cheerful and efficient liaison with the Old Globe; to Jack O'Brien, Craig Noel, and Tom Hall, who run the Old Globe with an artistry, enthusiasm, and skill unsurpassed by any theatrical-producing team in America. Thanks to my director, cast, and crew, and to the members of the Antaeus Company in Los Angeles, who saw it through its first readings. Thanks to the librarians at the Main Branch of the Los Angeles Public Library, who were always generous with their time and suggestions, and who went out of their way to procure books for me during the difficult months after the fire when their collections were dispersed or damaged and they were lodged in the cramped quarters in their temporary home. Thanks to my students, teachers, and colleagues at California State University, Hayward, where I studied and taught for so many years. Thanks to Steve Wozniak, Steve Jobs, and John Scully for overseeing the development of the Apples and Macintoshes that make writing and revising so much easier than anyone ever thought possible.

And thanks, of course, to my family, especially to my wife Anne McNaughton, from whom I stole so many hours to be with Moreto, but with whom I spent so many more hours, learning together about the theatre, about criticism, about playwriting, and in particular about the jobs and challenges of putting together a critical edition of a play. I worked as a typist for her on an earlier project and look forward to many more such projects together in the future.

Los Angeles, 1995

Contents

Forword

Nearly ten years ago, I found myself on a commuter jet flying between Toronto, where I was shooting the American Playhouse production of Arthur Miler's *All My Sons*, and New York. Next to me on the plane was the famed and often feared drama critic, John Simon, whom I had met briefly a year or so earlier. This side of a cobra and mongoose, there are few social combinations more volatile than a drama critic and a director, but in this case, we passed the time in flight without axes to grind, and only good conversation to share.

John, aware that I am Artistic Director of the Old Globe Theater in San Diego, lamented the paucity of world drama on American stages. With the exception of Molière, Calderon, and Chekhov, he felt that the world's greatest stage literature is virtually ignored in this country.

He mentioned *El desden con el desden* by Agustín Moreto as an example, and briefly and unforgettably he sketched out the classic situation of this great and resonating comedy. Small cast. Brief music. Hilarious and challenging roles. In every way, a sure-fire "hit." Long after we parted company, the idea of this "lost" classic lingered, appealing to me ever more.

I have spent some extended time with Dakin Matthews, initially as an actor, at the Globe, and then as a director, and finally as a brilliant dramaturge, whereupon I found myself naturally drawn to mention it to him. The term "Renaissance figure" is overused these days, but Dakin Matthews qualifies. His vast experience in theatre, his intellectual capacity for total conception, and his insatiable curiosity were immediately called into play, and it wasn't a matter of weeks before he embarked on translation and adaption which soon emerged as *Spite for Spite*.

The happy result follows, a warm, witty, lighter-than-air translation/adaptation of a work which must surely find its way into the mainstream of production in this country at long last.

Jack O'Brien Artistic Director
Old Globe Theatre San Diego, California

Introduction

Agustín Moreto
His Life

Agustín Moreto y Cavana was born in Madrid in early April, 1618, of Italian descent, his well-to-do parents, Agustín and Violante, having emigrated from Milan, or perhaps from Florence.

Young Agustín attended the University of Alcalá de Henares between 1634 and 1637, studying logic and physics and receiving his Licentiate in 1639. By 1643, he had been ordained a cleric in minor orders, with a benefice, and had also in all probability begun his dramatic writing.

By the middle of the century he was already a recognized literary figure and a member of the *Academia Castellana*. He published the first volume of his comedies (called the *Primera Parte*) in 1654; *El desdén, con el desdén* (literally "Disdain with Disdain"), one of his most popular and famous comedies, first appeared in print in this edition.

Sometime after 1657, Agustín was ordained a priest, at which time he seems to have cut back on, but not altogether ceased, his dramatic activity. He certainly wrote religious plays with some regularity for the rest of his life. Ruth Lee Kennedy surmises that perhaps he did write a few "secular" plays while he was a priest, but only for presentation at court and not in the public theatres. (27) He became a protege and chaplain of the Archbishop of Toledo, don Baltasar de Morosco y Sandoval, and at his request, entered the Brotherhood of San Pedro in 1659 in order to help administer the Hospital of San Nicolás. He lived on the Hospital grounds until his death ten years later in October of 1669, of an illness that left his final work, a play about St. Rose of Lima, unfinished. In his will he requested burial in the Hospital cemetery, a final wish that was not granted by his executors; he was buried instead in the Church of St. John the Baptist in Toledo.[1]

HIS LITERARY REPUTATION

Moreto is almost unknown today outside the Spanish-speaking world, though he must rank, after Lope de Vega and Calderón, as one of the brightest comedic lights of the Golden Age of Spanish Theatre. Even in the Spanish-speaking world, Moreto's fame has been to a certain extent qualified by an old and fairly ridiculous charge of plagiarism leveled against him for borrowing most of his plots from previous authors. Anyone acquainted with Renaissance literary theory and practice knows how feeble such a charge is, inasmuch as it could be applied to virtually anyone who wrote plays in the sixteenth and seventeenth centuries, including the mighty Shakespeare himself.[2] On top of which, Moreto—again like Shakespeare—almost unfailingly improves upon everything he borrows. And, on top of that, when it comes to the crime of borrowing, he is perhaps more sinned against than sinning, having been plundered more than once by European luminaries in search of scripts, including Gozzi, Marivaux, and no less than Molière himself, whose *The Princess of Elide* is a rewrite, in some places a straight translation, of *El desdén, con el desdén*.[3]

HIS WORKS

Like most dramatic writers of his day, Moreto wrote in a number of styles, some more successfully than others. His plays may be divided into the traditional Golden Age groupings of secular plays (comedies, histories, cape-and-sword plays), religious plays (saints plays, biblical plays, and shrine plays), and miscellaneous short pieces.

He himself oversaw the publication of the *Primera Parte,* containing twelve plays. The remaining editions of his work, some of them containing spurious attributions, were published posthumously, and include a second edition of the *Primera Parte* (1677), two editions of a *Secunda Parte* (1676), and a *Tercera Parte* (1681). In addition, some of his plays, some of his collaborations, and some pieces wrongly attributed to him appeared in a series of drama anthologies published in Madrid from 1652 to 1704, known collectively by its shortened title, *Escogidas*.

At present, critical opinion, mostly in the person of the world's acknowledged Moreto expert Ruth Lee Kennedy, has set the Moreto canon at "thirty-three plays written by Moreto alone, nineteen collaborations, and six of doubtful authenticity." (Castañeda 35) Of these, surely the best known, and those upon which Moreto's reputation is largely built, are the courtship comedy *El desdén, con el desdén* and the fop comedy *El lindo don Diego* ("Don Diego the Dandy").

His Dramatic Virtues

Most critics agree upon Moreto's strengths as a playwright.

The first is his skill at organization. When he borrows plots, his improvements are almost always those of regularizing and improving structure. Extraneous incidents are eliminated. Strong links are forged between subplot and plot, even and especially between the comic subplots and the more serious main plots. Logic and rationality dominate story, characterization, and language. Motivations and outcomes are coherent with behavior. There is a strong bias for the natural over the merely theatrical, both in action and language. Scenes and acts are cleanly begun, elegantly explored, and logically brought to their climaxes and conclusions.

The second, not unrelated, strength is his genius for comedy. All his structural skills clean and clarify the humor of the central story. The consistency of his characters, even his eccentric characters, makes them all the funnier for their believability. The logic of his plotting makes for highly polished comic effects both in the elegant scenes of intrigue and in the more farcical and satirical moments. His light touch with language makes him surely the wittiest of the Spanish comedians. And he is particularly successful in his re-fashioning and perfecting of the clown character (the *gracioso*) of Golden Age Theatre. Moreto is perhaps the first to have truly funny clowns who are never low in their humor nor extraneous in their function. In his integration of comic subplotting into the main plot line, he is unsurpassed in classical Spanish theatre and approaches Shakespeare himself.

The third is his gift for language and versification. His amazingly straightforward style avoids all excesses in literary language, no mean feat in an age which worshipped the baroqueries of Calderón and was only a generation removed from the exuberant decadence of "gongorism"—so named after its founder and most famous practitioner Luis de Góngora (d. 1627), a figure whom English readers might most easily appreciate if they imagine his rococo style to be a kind of hybrid of bad Metaphysical Poetry and unbridled Euphemism.[4]

His verse skills are as ingenious as they are varied. In the same play, he writes in a number of stanzaic forms; and even the most complicated seem, for the most part, effortless. His dominant verse form, the octosyllabic ballad rhyme, can run into hundreds and hundreds of lines, and yet seem perfectly natural. The English-speaking theatre has nothing to compare to it, really, since English is a relatively uninflected language, and the Spanish ballad rhyme (called *romance*) is really more assonance than rhyme and depends heavily on the similarity of inflections. In addition, the tradition of writing plays containing so many different lyric forms is particularly un-English—except perhaps in the musical comedy. So it is difficult for one raised in the English dramatic tradition to evaluate Moreto's skills accurately and to know just how much of a genius or innovator or merely skilled practitioner he was. Though the informed critical opinion is that he was a pleasant and skillful, but not particularly regular, dazzling, or ground-breaking versifier, to the average English-speaking reader or listener, his technical achievements seem almost staggering.

His fourth strength is his thematic consistency: as he was rational in his plotting, characterization, and language, so did he emphasize rationality in his view of the world. He was critical without being cruel, accepting rather than rejecting, and sought always to elevate his audience (while he was entertaining them) with a reasonableness rather untypical of his fellow Golden Age playwrights. There is little brutality or roughness in his plays, little excessive emotionalism, either sentimental or sadistic. His powerful common sense and his view of the world as essentially, or at least potentially, reasonable may account for his weakness at tragedy, but it makes for great comic strength. It curtails the tendency toward crude theatrical exaggeration so common to his stage, and helps both him and his audiences to see the human condition a bit more clearly and optimistically.

El desdén, con el desdén
THE SOURCES

Moreto's comedy first appeared in the *Primera Parte* in 1654. Mabel Harlan has made an exhaustive study of Moreto's possible sources and has come up with twenty earlier *comedias* to which *El desdén* may have been in some measure indebted. The closest, and almost undeniable one is, according to Narciso Cortés, Lope de Vega's *La vengadora de las mujeres* ("The Women's Revenge"). (Cortés xvi) But as Cortés points out, though the initial dramatic impulse may have been borrowed, as well as the basic structure—an unwilling woman and three suitors (in the original, from Transylvania, Albania, and Ferrara)—most everything else is greatly changed, and much for the better. The motivation is clearer, the psychology more natural, the humor both lighter and deeper, and the development of the action much more sophisticated and logical.

In Kennedy's view, the most likely path of influence can be traced from this Lope de Vega play and one other, *Los milagros del desprecio* ("Scorn Can Work Miracles"), through two of Moreto's earlier efforts, *El poder de la amistad* ("The Power of Friendship") and *Hacer remedio el dolor* ("A Prescription for Pain"). There are enough points of contact between these two plays and *El desdén* to suggest, in Kennedy's words, that the last play is "but the happy flowering of the other two." (161–165)

Other than that, no further sources really need be consulted, since the tale and the theme are almost commonplaces in Renaissance literature, with Moreto's treatment falling about halfway between Shakespeare's two great explorations of the theme: the Kate and Petruchio plot of *The Taming of the Shrew* and the Beatrice and Benedick subplot of *Much Ado About Nothing*.

Diana, the daughter of the Count of Barcelona, is both an heiress and a beauty, who nonetheless will not be wooed. Her father hopes that the appearance of three suitors and their gallantries will change her mind; and indeed the three—Carlos, the Count of Urgel; Gastón, the Count of Fox; and the unnamed Prince of Bearne—do all they can to oblige her to respond, but she refuses even to grace their courtesy with any more than the barest formality.

Instead, she and her ladies—Cintia, Laura, and Fenisa—keep court like the mythical Diana and her chaste nymphs, studying literature and legend for further confirmation of the uncertainties of love and the untrustworthiness of men. Diana keeps herself aloof from even the smallest signs of graciousness towards men, for fear of what they might lead to, and keeps equally close guard over her ladies when any of them shows signs of straying.

Carlos, especially, suffers from her disdain, for he has come not to woo but to wonder, only to find himself stricken by love like a thunderbolt. He confesses his infatuation to his recently arrived man, Polilla ("Moth"), who engineers a series of plots to gain the lady's love—all of which depend upon Carlos's treating her with equal disdain. Hence, the title, which translates perhaps more accurately as "Disdain (Cured) With Disdain."

First, Polilla insinuates himself into Diana's household and obtains employment as her jester under the name of Caniquí ("cotton cloth"). Then, when Diana, at her father's insistence, finally confronts the three suitors, Carlos seconds her attack on love and marriage and reveals that he himself has taken a similar vow not to love, or even to be loved. Diana is first fascinated, then horrified to discover that she has no power over this man; and at the prompting of Polilla, embarks on a plan of revenge. She will try to test his resolve by making him fall in love with her.

To accomplish this, she manages underhandedly to gain Carlos as her partner in the Carnival celebrations going on in Barcelona. In the other pairings, done—not quite by chance—through the "ceremony of the colors," Bearne gets Cintia, Gastón gets Fenisa, and Polilla gets Laura. As the couples go off to dance, Carlos, after confessing to Polilla and the audience how hard it is to keep up the pretense, goes on to offend Diana further by his diffidence, till she dismisses him in a rage. Then she confides in Polilla her plan to trap Carlos into love by having him brought secretly into her garden where he will hear her singing, an experience Polilla assures her will turn the poor man "to jelly."

Then when Diana has left, Polilla instructs Carlos to ignore her completely in the garden and pretend to be a great admirer of everything there—the landscaping, the architecture, the view—everything, that is, except the lady's singing. Carlos barely manages to pull this deception off—with the help of some pointed threats from Polilla—and Diana is cast into a fury which even she suspects is beginning to feel a lot like love.

So she and Polilla plot a second stratagem—jealousy. Diana is to reveal to Carlos that she has changed her mind and will now give herself over to love and marriage, since she has found such a noble and gallant suitor—in Bearne. Carlos is momentarily stunned, but recovers with an announcement of his own engagement: he too has fallen in love and is about to ask Cintia for her hand. He rushes out to congratulate Bearne, and Diana in his absence erupts into a passion, castigating herself for being a fool, and Love for making her one.

When Bearne returns to thank her for her favor, she treats him rudely, which he seems barely to notice, so great is his happiness. And when Cintia asks her permission to wed Carlos, Diana's passion turns to a frenzy of confession, outrage, and despair. Cintia, aware now of exactly what is going on, approaches Carlos and tells him the truth—that Diana loves him and that he need not remain faithful to his earlier proposal if he wishes to return that love. Diana hides herself to overhear her father and the Princes making plans for a double wedding, and Carlos, aware of her overhearing, makes a passionate, but well-reasoned speech, placing his own will at Diana's mercy. She reveals herself, gains from her father a promise to honor her wishes, and chooses Carlos for her husband. Bearne good-naturedly chooses Cintia, and Laura snags "Caniquí," who reveals himself laughingly as Polilla and begs the company's—and the audience's—pardon.

THE STRUCTURE

El desdén, con el desdén is written in the traditional form of the Golden Age, in three acts with no scene divisions. (Later such scenic divisions were added by some editors following classical French models.) The three acts are also, to a certain extent, three days; the Spanish word for an act of a play is in fact *jornada,* or "day." The three are roughly equal in length—about a thousand lines of verse each. All three acts use music effectively to comment upon the action. And all three are also markedly different in comic structure—the first emphasizing debate; the second, comic action; and the third, surprise and self-revelation.

ACT ONE. As is typical of Moreto's practice, the exposition is done early in the first act by a long speech—in this case, Carlos's amazing 328-line description to Polilla of his current desperate love for Diana. (Only very early and very late did Shakespeare try this expository strategy—in *The Comedy of Errors* and *The Tempest.*) Also typical of Moreto's comedy is the comic counterpoint between Carlos's seriousness and Polilla's punning and satirical commentary.

At this point the rest of the male characters are introduced, with the entrance of the father and the other two suitors. Their description of Diana's stubborn disdain is again counterpointed by Polilla's running commentary and interjections; and at the end of their discussion, Carlos announces to them his intention to accompany them on their mission to confront Diana. Then when they have gone, he confides in Polilla that he has a plan to conquer Diana's disdain. What the plan is, is unclear at this point; but it does involve two things: Polilla's assistance in infiltrating Diana's court, and Carlos's own public denial of any amorous intentions toward the lady. With that, the stage clears, to prepare for the introduction of the female characters.

Again, rather typically, Moreto uses music to introduce and comment upon the central action.[5] Accompanied by musicians, the ladies enter and immediately begin to debate the issue of love and courtship. Diana takes sides against both—against love for its tyranny, and against courtship for the inevitable invitation it issues to love. Arguing against Diana is her rather more practical cousin Cintia, who maintains that love cannot be that bad, since it is natural, and further that courtship is merely refined courtesy which need be neither feared nor avoided. (In so doing, she rather reminds one of Berowne—to Diana's Navarre—in a similar debate in *Love's Labour's Lost,* though of course in the Shakespeare, it is the men, not the women, who vow to establish their little court of chastity.)

The debate structure of this section of the act is again typical of Moreto and allows him to be philosophical, as is his wont, and to place Diana and her ladies rather firmly in the seventeenth-century *précieux* mode. Thus he can explore the central issue of the play with reasoned arguments and sophisticated intellectualism; and on top of that, he can rescue his heroine Diana from silliness and vapidity—as well as from irrationality—by subtlety, seriousness, and articulateness with which he graces her.

At this point, Polilla enters, now in disguise and wearing professorial robes, to seek employment in Diana's court. The clown as mock-expert is a typical *gracioso* strategy, here brought to comic perfection by Moreto's wittiness. Polilla's fooling is full both of puns and barbs, and his pose as a "Doctor of Love" allows him to satirize (and cure) Diana's unwillingness to love even as he ingratiates himself with her. He plays a part not unlike Feste's to Olivia in the opening scenes of *Twelfth Night*, both to amuse and mock her; and his proposed curative expertise reminds one of Rosalind's similar exercise with Orlando in the Ganymede scenes of *As You Like It*.

The men invade the women's domain rather abruptly with the entrance of the Count of Barcelona and the three suitors. Three further debates ensue. The first is between father and daughter over obedience and love, in which the father ends up rather firmly on the losing side. The second is between Diana and Bearne (who acts as spokesman for the suitors) over the reasonableness or unreasonableness of loving; the conclusion of that debate is Diana's acceptance of the wooers' challenge to oppose their gallantry to her disdain and see which one wins.

The third debate is the more extended one, and the first onstage joust between the two protagonists, Carlos and Diana. The subject of the debate is not just loving, but being loved as well. Carlos first maintains that his presence at the gallantries is a courtesy only, and has nothing to do with courtship or love. And Carlos further affirms that his own distaste for love is so great that he will not even permit himself to be loved, since that leads inevitably to discourtesy on the part of the unwilling beloved and heartbreak on the part of the insistent lover. His diffidence piques Diana, who resolves to teach this cold suitor a suitable lesson. She exits, and Polilla assures the nearly despairing Carlos that their stratagem will work, in fact is working, even as the act closes.

ACT TWO. Like the first act, the second act begins with a set speech of exposition, as Polilla narrates to Carlos the progress of their plot. He has become not only Diana's clown, but her confidante as well, and can assure Carlos that the lady has been "bitten" by love. The stratagem of returning disdain will work, if only Carlos can keep it up. When Carlos asks for proof, Polilla offers the fact that Diana has decided to use the upcoming Carnival festivities as an occasion for pairing up with him to take her revenge for his disdain. There follows a description of the "ceremony of the colors," by which men choose their partners for the feast by chance.

Carlos then hides, as Diana and her ladies enter; and they too discuss the "ceremony," as Diana plots to pre-empt the luck of the draw and gain Carlos for her partner. She then confides in Polilla, and asks him if her plan is likely to work; Polilla, acting as a double agent for Carlos, promises her that it will, even as he almost immediately assures the hidden Carlos that their double-cross will work. And all the time, Polilla acts as a kind of triple agent for the audience, to whom he comments—in witty asides—on the progress of the action as if it were a game of cards or bowls he were observing and announcing.

There is next a debate between the two protagonists, in which both try to outdo one another in analyzing and justifying their disdain, and to which Polilla provides another running commentary, deflating both of them. The debate climaxes with Carlos's impassioned disquisition on the follies and dangers of loving, which has the unexpected result of making Diana rush, rather uncharacteristically, to love's defense. In that slightly confused state, Diana hears the music heralding the entrance of the suitors, and the "ceremony of the colors" begins.

This ritual is the centerpiece of the play and of the second act, falling almost exactly midway in both. (For the climax to be at virtually the mathematical midpoint of the play is typical of Moreto's structure.[6]) Also typical is the use of music not only to introduce, but to comment upon the action, as the lyrics of each verse make rather pointed comments about the ceremony in general and the individual choices in particular. And once again, Polilla's satirical participation in the ceremony offers a comic gloss on the rhetoric of the serious suitors, as he not only mocks their selection speeches but their high flown compliments as well with his own self-deprecating and ridiculous responses.

As the pairs promenade off to the next room, Diana and Carlos hesitate at the door, masked and hand in hand, for another exchange. In perhaps their cleverest scene together, they both find themselves nearly unable to control the growing love they have for one another. Carlos is the first to let his mask fall, when he takes Diana's invitation to flirt seriously and passionately confesses his desperate love for her. Just as she drops her mask and is about to take her cruel revenge on him, he catches himself and pretends that it was all in jest, merely to fulfill his Carnival obligation to pay court to his lady for the day. She is now caught off guard, since she took his protestations as seriously as he had made them, and finds herself now in a state of confusion—somewhere between humiliation and disappointment. She orders him out of her sight, a command he pretends to obey only too willingly, and she nearly collapses under the strain.

Polilla comes in to find her distressed, and, with his help, she hatches yet another plot: to have Carlos brought secretly into her garden where he can hear her singing and so be entranced by her. Polilla swears to do his part, and then once she has gone, reveals the whole plan to Carlos, who at the first sound of her singing is nonetheless hopelessly bewitched; and it is only by sheer willpower and physical threats that Polilla is able to force his master to go through with the continuing charade of indifference.

Once again the ladies sing—this time a deliberately sentimental and romantic song—rather like the one Orsino requests in *Twelfth Night* to sate his greedy amorousness: "That old and antic song we heard last night/Methought it did relieve my passion much." (*TN* 2.4.3–4) And to this slightly overripe ballad, master and man stroll about the garden commenting on everything *but* the ladies' singing. Diana is driven nearly mad with frustration, dispatching messenger after messenger to get Carlos's attention; and when at last he feigns seeing her for the first time, she orders him out for his insolence, dismisses her ladies, and rants on to her only confidante, Polilla, about her desperate state. And at Polilla's gleeful comment upon the success of the plot, the act ends.

So where the first act was almost exclusively conversational, the second act translates the substance of those exchanges into actions—into ceremonies, dances, songs, overhearings, and physical passes and crossings of the stage. At the same time, the controlled intellectuality of the first act is transformed into less controllable passion in the second act, as both protagonists find their emotions running away with them, and Polilla must act both as restraining force and comic commentator on their runaway love. As Polilla notes at the end of the second act, the courtship has become something of a dance, and a slightly wild one at that.

ACT THREE. There is virtually no debate in the third act. The intellectual issues of the play have been thoroughly laid out in the first two acts; both sides have had their chance to argue, and the theme has been exhaustively explored in language. What happens in the third act is the resolution of the actual conflict through action, coupled with an extensive, and simultaneously funny and touching self-exploration by Diana of her own mental and emotional state.

The act begins with typical Moretan exposition. The two spurned suitors, Bearne and Gastón, rather too lately hit upon what they think is an original plan for melting Diana's resistance—they will ignore her; and they ask Carlos to do the same. As Polilla points out, this plays right into Carlos's plans as well; for Diana is, according to Polilla's close observation, very definitely on the verge of crumbling. Polilla also tips Diana's latest plot, which is to rouse Carlos to jealousy as a way of punishing him; all Carlos has to do, warns Polilla, is ignore her attempts.

This expository beginning thus sets up the comedy of the rest of the act in a very obvious, but nonetheless efficient fashion. All the characters, by means of conversations with other characters, let the audience know exactly what they intend to do. Then when the audience sees them do it, there is first the laugh of recognition, followed quickly by the laugh of irony—inasmuch as the audience knows more than the characters on whom the various tricks are being played. And then comes the laugh of superiority, when even the forewarned characters fail to avoid the trap, and then the laugh of surprise as they improvise their way out of it. And through it all, the audience is guided by the *gracioso's* running commentary.

The action proper of the act starts with the sound of music and the entrance of Diana. The songs offstage are the love-songs written by Bearne and Gastón in praise of their ladies Cintia and Fenisa. Even Polilla gets into the act with a mocking lyric of praise for his chosen lady Laura. Diana protests she cannot bear to hear such drivel, yet wonders why Carlos has written her no such song. Polilla assures her that he would have, if only he could have fallen in love. But he cannot and will not, even though he intends to insist upon showing up for the festivities and partnering her.

At this point, the three suitors enter and, as previously plotted, ignore Diana completely. She confronts Carlos about his neglect of her, and then slides neatly into her plot. She announces that she really needs to talk to him because he is the expert, and she values his opinion. She has decided, she says, to fall in love and marry; in fact, she has already chosen her prospective mate, Bearne, whom she praises to the skies. Carlos, though warned of this stratagem, falls for it anyway; and only at Polilla's insistent goading does he manage to improvise a counterplot; he too has fallen in love, with the most beautiful woman he has ever seen—who else but Diana's cousin Cintia.

Diana collapses into shock, then into outrage, as Carlos describes the wonders of Cintia in a passionate lover's declaration, and then meets all Diana's objections point for point before rushing off to propose to the lady and congratulate Bearne on his good fortune. Diana is left first to complain to and confide in Polilla, who all but mocks her to her face, and then, in a sonnet, to berate her own heart for its weakness and folly.

Bearne interrupts this passionate musing, bounding in in a fit of elation over the news he has just heard, and Diana dismisses him rudely but to little effect. Diana is torn between the need to voice her agony of love and to keep silent, when her cousin Cintia enters to beg her permission to wed. And then Diana, in a lengthy and amazing speech of passionate self-revelation, at once hilarious and deeply moving, confesses all to Cintia and rushes from the stage humiliated and in distress. Cintia finds Carlos, and confesses what she has heard to him, offering to withdraw from the match if it suits Carlos.

The denouement is typically swift. The men enter, discussing the prospects of a double marriage. Diana hides behind a curtain to overhear what she assumes will be her final defeat. Polilla sees her and urges Carlos to make one final speech which will persuade both the happy father and the concealed daughter of his true intentions and resolve everything. He does so, and Diana reveals herself to claim Carlos for a husband. Amidst the general rejoicing, other couples pair off, and Polilla reveals his true identity.

Overall, then, the structure of the play emphasizes balance and symmetry rather than copiousness and bizzarreness. By the middle of the first act, all the characters of the play have been introduced; there will be no new ones after that. Nor—for all practical purposes—will there be any unexpected or sudden occurrences. The twists and turns of the plot are achieved with precise logic; the development is more ingenious than inspired, more mathematical than miraculous. Yet it is never mechanical. The payoff is in the concentration of the comic action, the intensity of the debate, and the clarification of the protagonists' mental and emotional states. This last marks a psychological advance for Golden Age comedy, and one which Moreto to a great extent pioneered.[7]

The three principal characters of the comedy—Diana, Carlos, and Polilla—are all fairly typical of Moreto's work, though perhaps nowhere else do they achieve the level of comic perfection they enjoy in *El desdén*. Of the two lovers, it is important to note that for all their singleness of purpose, neither is ever one-dimensional. In other plays—called by critics *comedias de figurón*—Moreto shows himself quite capable of the broad strokes and character exaggerations that English audiences easily recognize in their own comedies of humours and manners. And undeniably, Moreto has concentrated his characterization of these two upon a dominant trait overthrown by love—Carlos's pride, Diana's disdain. But in both cases, he takes great care to give each lover a level of psychological reality and self-awareness—and especially of self-mockery—that makes them alive and rounded and (very importantly) eminently likeable.

DIANA: Diana is neither stupid nor cold. Her pose of disdain is a choice she voluntarily makes, based on her careful reading and continuous musing about the dangers of love. That she is capable of logical thinking and clever persuasion we know from the early part of the play. That she is capable of great passion we know from the end. Her virtue and her vice blend almost seamlessly into one another. In her aristocratic birth and self-possession she is a typical Moreto heroine. If she is over-cautious, a *précieux* even, one need only look at the fate her world normally held in store for bright, wealthy women to find her caution justified. Indeed, if all her suitors were as vapid and indistinguishable as Bearne and Gastón—the Rosencrantz and Guildenstern of courtship, as it were—one would certainly side with the lady's reticence. And one need only look at portrayals of marriageable women by virtually any other Golden Age playwright to see how unique and understanding Moreto is in creating his female characters.

Given the artificial nature of the comedy, Diana's development from disdainful woman to committed lover is carefully and delightfully detailed by the playwright. (Compare the relative suddenness of the conversion of her two sisters in English drama, Katherine and Beatrice—the one by exhaustion and the other by deception—and you will have some idea of just how carefully and accurately Moreto has charted her course.) First there is little more than the joy of besting a disdainful male in debate, and then the astonishment at finding him holding his position so tenaciously, then the decision to exact a kind of intellectual revenge on a fool. There is, of course, more than a little hurt female pride involved from the very beginning, but neither Diana nor the audience is made particularly aware of that.

The next stage, as related by Polilla, is clearly a growing fascination with the disdainful Carlos; this is followed by the kind of public humiliation in the Carnival festivities that touches her right where she is most vulnerable—at her sense of self-worth and decorum. Her desire for revenge now becomes personal, and as such makes her even more vulnerable. She risks very much playing the fool in the garden scene where she abandons all pretense of an intellectual victory and seeks instead to conquer Carlos with her charms; and when these (apparently) fail her, she senses (quite rightly) that even her own women are laughing at her behind her back.

In the third act, Diana is practically frantic with her frustration. Even the disdain of Bearne and Gastón irks her; and her best strategy—the jealousy card—is trumped by Carlos's counterplay. She is left with nothing but her pain, as even she begins to see—and her self-knowledge and self-mockery are the very things that endear her to us—that what she feels is undeniably love. It is an experience so new to her she cannot even give it a name, or would prefer not to, since the only name she knows—love—is so hateful to her. But love it is, and love she must confess in her two amazing monologues to Cintia. Her confession is so complete, her humiliation so total, that the audience can only forgive her, and rejoice with her when she sees her defeat transformed in a moment to victory. She exits the play graciously and wittily, and somehow we know that these two antagonists are perfect matches for one another.

CARLOS: Carlos is also typical of Moreto's young heroes; he is, of course, well-born, proud, valiant, and generous, but without the more extreme vices of cruelty, boasting, greed, and erratic behavior that typify many of his peers in the work of other Golden Age dramatists. He is rather, as Kennedy capsulizes him, very much "the courteous gentlemen whose morals are as irreproachable as his manners" (77); "not far from the idealized 'decent chap' of the past century, so dear to the hearts of Victorian readers." (80).

Moreto does not give him the benefit of the kind of dramatic development that he gives Diana, except insofar as that development is related by the principal himself. This is the major difference between Carlos and Diana, and one of the comic strengths of the structure of the play. What happens to Diana over the course of the play is essentially what *happened* to Carlos before the play began. He is, at the beginning of the piece, hopelessly in love and he knows it; he must learn to control it if he wishes to win the lady. She is not in love, but she will grow to be; and as she does, she will know it only gradually; and in a real sense she must learn to lose control in order to get her man.

Diana *lives out* her development; Carlos *narrates* his. But in that wonderful 328-line monologue, he *re*-lives his conversion with such energy and such humor, both intentional and unintentional, that we are finally charmed by him. And over the course of the play, he is such a victim of his own passion, and such a pawn to Polilla's manipulation, that we find his innocent boyishness finally winning. And we are relieved when he manages—at the crucial moments and after much prompting—to hit on exactly the right speech to win the day.

POLILLA: Kennedy identifies in Moreto two basic *gracioso* types, whom she calls the "Plautean" and the "rustic Sancho":

> The one is the product of the city and its trickery; the other is rooted in the soil and simplicity of the country village. The one is given to Latin phrases and constant punning; the other to colloquial pronunciations and felicitous malapropisms of speech. The one secretly rejoices in an intellectual power which enables him to direct the destinies of those who are his social superiors; the other plumes himself on an importance in this world which he in no wise possesses. The one is frequently satiric at the expense of humanity in general and of lovers in particular; the other knows little of people and is, in some instances, at the mercy of a capricious young serving girl. (85)

Clearly, Polilla belongs to the first type. And with his homey comparisons, almost always to food or games, he deflates and mocks the pretensions both of lovers and of experts. There is only the barest subplot in his Carnival wooing and winning of Laura, a subplot which exists only to give him occasion to parody the rhetoric and self-deceptions of his betters.

In his ongoing asides to the audience, as well as in his stage management of the principal action of the play, he is a close cousin of the Vice character of early English drama, both direct descendants of the mischievous minor devil of the Corpus Christi and Morality plays.[8] His language is direct, colloquial, and at times earthy. There is even the possibility that his language may be earthier than we know, given our relative ignorance of seventeenth-century low slang. At least that is the opinion of Edward M. Wilson and Duncan Moir, who cite Bances Candamo's 1690 history of seventeenth-century Spanish theatre to back their observation:

> *Don Agustín Moreto fue quien estragó la pureza del teatro, con poco reparadas graciosidades, dejándose arrastrar del vulgar aplauso del pueblo....* [Don Agustín Moreto was one who corrupted the purity of the theatre with fooleries that have little to recommend them, debasing himself to gain the vulgar applause of the public.] It may be that the patent moral integrity of many of Moreto's main characters so dazzles us that, with our imperfect knowledge of seventeenth-century slang and innuendo, we fail to detect a certain scurrility in some of his graciosos and jokes. (128–129; translation mine)

But it may also be, as the two go on to point out, more of an aesthetic than an ethical repugnance on Bances Candamo's part to Moreto's dramatic style, rather like Sir Philip Sidney's famous criticism of the mixing of kings and clowns in the theatre of his day.

THE IDEAS

In her analysis of Moreto's work, Kennedy divides his secular comedies into two basic types: plays of plot and play of character and idea; and in the latter category are at least two further subtypes; *comedias de figurón,* or comedies of exaggerated character; and comedies where character is less exaggerated and ideas are prominent. (13–16) For all its wonderful characterization, *El desdén* must be classed as a comedy of ideas.

One of its ideas is clearly the opposition of disdain and love. This is so constant a theme in Moreto's work that Kennedy suggests it must have had roots deep in Moreto's own character. (110–111) Part of Moreto's treatment focuses on the psychological sources of love and disdain, sources which are discussed with the philosophical precision of a Medieval Schoolman, which is to some extent what Moreto, trained in a Spanish university, advanced into orders, and finally ordained a priest, was bound to be. Aristotelian and Thomistic concepts like reason, free will, affection, passion, nature, happiness are not tossed about casually; there is, especially in the early part of the play, almost a feeling of a university debate, a session of *quaestiones adlibitum,* with terms clearly defined and argument and counterargument carefully marshaled.

There is a healthy dose of didacticism in this play, and in Moreto's plays generally—fortunately, almost always an entertaining didacticism. There is also a nearly total avoidance of some of the most popular themes and situations of Golden Age drama—death, the grotesque, passionate patriotism, dangerous sexuality, an exaggerated and often fatal sense of honor *(pundonor).* In their stead are the themes of courtesy, generosity, and especially rationality. Indeed, virtually all Moreto's works seem composed to affirm two truths: that virtue is man's end, and that reason is the path to virtue.

Thus it is astonishing to find the author, in perhaps his greatest play, puzzling over the very human truth that love conquers all, even reason; and that happiness seems to depend more on love than on virtue. Perhaps that is what gives the comedy its special piquancy. It is certainly a theme that has a bit of a Shakespearean ring to it; and, in the end, it is not all that foreign to the very practical and commonsensical side of Moreto's artistic nature.

THE STAGING

It would seem that in the time of Moreto, the really spectacular stage effects—and there were plenty—were reserved for religious plays and court plays, and that the comedies performed in the public theatres (called *corrales*) were relatively uncluttered in the matter of stagecraft and setting. Like their cousins in the English theatre, Spanish players tended to work in gorgeous costumes (often hand-me-downs from aristocrats) but on bare stages. The playing platform itself was unlocalized space, until and unless the characters identified it as somewhere definite. There was generally little or no actual scenery. Entrances and exits were by means of doors, and a curtain may sometimes have been used for a discovery or for the swift and continuous move from one scene to another.[9]

As said before, Moreto himself divides his plays into acts, but not into scenes as such. In the two intervals between the acts, lapses of time almost always occur, just how much to be indicated as quickly as possible in the dialogue which begins the new act. This as least was Lope de Vega's suggestion in his 1609 poem *Arte neuvo de hacer comedias en este tiempo* ("The New Art of Making Plays Nowadays"), and Kennedy, among others, finds little evidence that much changed in this regard in Spanish public theatre between Lope and Moreto. (50) The idea that each act was a day was not strictly observed, certainly not in the more epic and historical pieces; but in the comedies generally, and in *El desdén* certainly, there was often a kind of loose observance of the unity of time.

The one dramaturgical precept of some interest is the practice of clearing the stage to indicate a change of locale. If the arrival or departure of a character generally signals a change of scene (the so-called "French scene," after neo-classical French practice), then there are between twenty-five and thirty-one such scenes in *El desdén* (depending upon just how loosely or strictly the rule is enforced); and many editors mark them that way. But, other than between acts, on only two occasions (ll. 547 and 1824) is the stage left momentarily vacant, and this in Moreto all but unfailingly means a change of locale. So as Kennedy points out, in all of *El desdén* there are only five locales (which some editors again insist on specifying), and only two instances of a change of locale within an act (45–50). This is economical stagecraft at its best.

A NOTE ON THE TEXT

For the record, I have used primarily the excellent Francisco Rico edition, published as part of the *Clásicos Castalia* series, copyrighted by *Editorial Castalia* in 1971. The misprints I have found there so far are: the faulty ascription of Diana's crucial speech beginning on line 828 to Polilla; the failure to properly ascribe half a line to Diana on line 1557; a miscounting of lines between 1470 and 1490, which results in mislineation of that section of the Rico edition of the play. I have also consulted the other modern editions listed in the bibliography.

The text of *Spite for Spite* has the traditional line-numbering of the early critical editions. Critical and dramatugical notes are at the end of the text; they are mine unless credited to another editor. If they are translated, the translation is mine unless otherwise credited. Textual and translator's notes also appear there when I have felt they were important or of interest—when, for example, something in the Spanish text is disputed or untranslatable, or when something in the translation is more mine than Moreto's.

I have used only Moreto's stage directions, or those of his earliest editors; there is no attempt in this edition to suggest a full staging of the play. I do not, however, use the scene breaks or scene descriptions favored by many editors; Rico is quite conservative in this matter, and I follow his lead. I also follow him in indenting the first lines of stanzas through the text; I find it helpful to the reader, and an efficient reminder of which of the many strophic forms we are in at any given time.

Notes

1. Further biographic information about Moreto may be found in Castañeda (pp. 15–20), Kennedy (pp. 1–7), and Cortés (pp. v–ix).
2. Kennedy points out that there was in Spain, during Moreto's time, a rather amazing law against originality in dramatic writing, which made it illegal to invent plots or depart from the accepted history or hagiography of the subject matter (75).
3. Further analyses of continental borrowings from Moreto may be found in Cortés (pp. xvii–xxii), Kennedy (pp. 118–119), and Castañeda (p. 83).
4. For more on Góngora, see Wilson and More (p. 121).
5. For more on Moreto's use of music, see Morley (pp. 163–164) and Casa (pp. 146–147).
6. This point is made, with further illustration, in Kennedy (p. 45).
7. For more on Moreto's contributions to psychological characterization in Golden Age drama, see Kennedy (pp. 88–94; 116–117), Casa (*passim*), and Casteñeda (*passim*).
8. The classic treatment of the development of the Vice character in English drama is Bernard Spivack, *Shakespeare and the Allegory of Evil* (New York, 1958).
9. For a full treatment of Golden Age stagecraft, see Rennert (pp. 76–103, *et passim*) and Shergold (*passim*).

SPITE FOR SPITE

Cast of Characters

CARLOS: Count of Urgel

POLILLA: (called Moth), a clown, and Carlos's man

The COUNT of Barcelona

The Prince of BEARNE

Don GASTÓN: the Count of Fox

DIANA: the daughter of the Count of Barcelona

her Ladies:
  CINTIA
  LAURA
  FENISA

MUSICIANS

Spite for Spite

(El desdén, con el desdén)

Act One
(Enter Carlos and Polilla.)

CARLOS:
 I must be going completely mad;
The woman's spiteful—that's all I can say!
POLILLA:
I've only just arrived today—
Tell me the troubles that you've had.
 I find you in Barcelona; you're   5
A local hero. All the town
Praises your courage up and down
And your conquests. And what's more,
 You're Carlos, Count of Urgel by birth,
Which adds to your fame and glory;   10
If they ever tried to write your story,
There's not enough paper on earth.
 Is there some reason I don't know about,
For getting yourself into such a stew?
Master, the more I think about you,   15
The less I can figure you out!
CARLOS:
 Oh, Moth, there's a lot more there
Than meets the eye. It's not just sadness,
That I'm feeling—it's more like madness,
Madness, slouching towards despair.   20

POLILLA:

Despair! Oh master, if you don't want to choke,
Hang on! Remember what despair
Did to the Apostle with the bright red hair!

CARLOS:

I'm suffering here, and you're making a joke!

POLILLA:

Who's joking? I'm trying to humor you.   25
But tell me, master, is there any hope?
Or are you at the end of your rope?

CARLOS:

I'm dying!

POLILLA:

       You're right, you're turning blue.
Hang on, master; give him some air!

CARLOS:

Don't mock me, boy, or I may get mad!   30

POLILLA:

I'm stringing you along, is that so bad?
Just trying to help a friend in despair.

CARLOS:

If you'll stop this clowning for half a minute
I'll tell you exactly where I hurt,
It's here, my heart. Oh. Moth, I'm cert-   35
ain you can relieve the pain that's in it,
If the past successes of your wit
Are any indication
Of your skill at medication.

POLILLA:

All right then, master, come on, spit   40
Out your passion—away with care!
Moth is here! Your trusty
Servant. Unlock the musty
Closet of your heart, and give it some air.

CARLOS:

You know I came here on vacation   45
And found in Barcelona, one name
On everyone's lips; they'd all proclaim

Their universal admiration
 Of a certain princess in this land,
Diana by name, whose beauty drew 50
So many lords and princes to
Vie for the pleasure of her hand.
 And so they did in a competition,
Of strength, of skill, of charm, of wit.
POLILLA:
I already know the rest of it. 55
You went to this little exhibition,
 Uninvited, just to play,
Just to give yourself a chance
To show off all your moves and fanc-
y medals, and of course you won the day.
CARLOS:
 But listen to my tale of woe! 60
POLILLA:
What? Did you fall in love?
CARLOS:
I did.
POLILLA:
         Whoa! I may never recov-
er from the shock.
CARLOS:
                      But listen!
POLILLA:
                        Go.
CARLOS:
 Remember back in dear Urgel 65
Before I left, the news went round
That Count Bearne and Count Fox
Were both in love? I later found
It was Diana that they wooed.
And their romancing brought her such fame, 70
That all the city sang her praises,
And all the country praised her name.
If love could so transform such princes,
Tame their excesses, make them meek,

(Such at least was the common tale) 75
That envy itself could only speak
Of them kindly, I had to see for myself.
Was it just courtesy, was it a case
Of personal taste, of rumor, or the force
Of heavenly beauty in Diana's face? 80
And so I came to Barcelona,
And showed up at her house one day.
Well, my heart didn't exactly stop,
And my face didn't give me away,
When I saw her. She was pretty enough, 85
A little too cool, not overripe
Or underfed, not coarse or common,
But not the exotically gorgeous type—
One of those little dears whose charms
Remain a mystery to all but the buck 90
Who loves her. Reason can only ascribe
It to *je ne sais quoi,* or just dumb luck.
So there I was, among the others,
Striving to prove myself braver
Than my rivals, in public displays 95
Of skill, all to win her favor.
My valor accomplished what love couldn't do;
I trotted out all my fanciest stuff,
I went to the tournaments and the feasts,
If it was required, I did more than enough, 100
Whatever I could in the cult of that goddess
Whose worship exacted the ultimate price—
Not love of course, no trace of that—
But other than love, any sacrifice.
As fate would have it, I always won. 105
In all their attempts they were beaten down
And crushed in every bout, and in all
Of mine I walked away with the crown.
And all the people shouted whenever
A garland was planted on my head, 110
You earned it, they all cheered to me,
When really it was luck instead—

Pure luck!—since either of the two
With whom I came to be a rival   115
Deserved to win far more than I.
But this was the secret of my survival:
It was the very absence of love,
Which freed me of cupidity;
So everything their hearts desired
Just fell in my lap quite naturally.   120
Because in matters of chance, you know,
Fate has a very nasty habit,
Of giving success to the very man
Who doesn't go out of his way to grab it.
Well, anyway, while all my praises   125
Were being sung and then re-sung,
One little girl, Diana by name,
Had the insolence to hold her tongue.
She's got a haughty disposition,
That one! this rather expensive display   130
Was undertaken for her approval
And she wouldn't give me the time of day!
I don't require a loving response—
But at least a simple think you, sir!
This was a haughtiness so cool   135
That any respect I had for her
Completely vanished out of sight.
This was too excessive to be
Simple composure, this went beyond
The boundaries of propriety,   140
This crossed the borders of mere reserve,
And arrived at sheer discourtesy.
A lady must walk a very fine line,
From which she must never waiver;
On the one side there's deliberate neglect   145
And on the other side, favor.
And etiquette requires of her
That she must carefully guide her foot
To touch neither one side nor the other.
If fondly she should slip and put   150

Her toe too far over the line
That marks the boundary of affection,
She cheapens herself. And if she veers
Too far in the opposite direction,
Trying too hard to avoid being gracious,   155
She ends up simply being rude.
And this was the *faux pas* Diana made:
She owed me a debt of gratitude,
Or at least she owed me her attention,
For the brilliant way in which I wooed.   160
As my commitment to these trials
Created in me a similar duty
To seek more tests of my valor and skill
To offer her back as a pledge of her beauty.
But what could I possibly make of behavior   165
Like hers, so standoffish and so cool,
Except to take it as cause for complaint
And clear proof that she's simply cruel?
Well, obviously it became my task
To find out the reason for her spite—   170
Some grudge or resentment, based on a mis-
reported or imaginary slight.
What I discovered was that Diana—
With all the power of her mind—
Had decided that philosophy   175
Was the highest wisdom she could find;
And from her studies and all her lessons
Had plucked this moral from the old Greek stories
That men in general were good for nothing
But scorn; and all the natural glories   180
Of the God of Love became the objects
Of her rage. Love—the very stone and lime
With which the world builds for itself
Palaces that stand to the end of time—
Love, in her unshakeable view,   185
Which like a sentence of death she gave,
Love was an all unworthy passion,
Which turned a woman into a slave.

So much so, that in spite of the fact
That she was an heiress and a princess born   190
And thus obliged to get herself wed,
She rejected her duty, and treated with scorn
The thought that any mere man should become
The master of her high estate.
Her rooms she made into the grove   195
Of divine Diana, and all her great
Ladies were nymphs, and in this fond
Conceit, she passed the livelong day.
She covered her walls with tapestries
Depicting the nymphs fleeing away   200
From love—images hung to engender
Disdain. Look over here, here's one
Of Daphne evading Apollo, or here,
Of Anaxárte turned to stone,
Because the poor thing wouldn't love.   205
Arethusa turned to a spring,
The bitter tears of her disdain
With Alpheus's tide commingling.
Well, once her father the Count had seen
How stubborn she was in her mistake,   210
How more so with each passing day,
How reason had no power to make
Her change her mind, nor all his pleas,
How cranky and irritable she grew
At the barest mention of the word love,   215
Which he feared might lead the poor girl to
A state of hopeless insanity,
He looked for a gentle remedy
(For he was ever a prudent man)
And to the neighboring princes sent he,   220
In hopes that the feast they staged for her,
The games they played, the jousts they fought,
Would have the effect that neither his pleas
Nor all his arguments had wrought,
And Nature would win out in the end.   225
At the sight of all that adulation,

Honor, service, duty, desire,.
Praise, affection, adoration,
She'd be overcome by her curiosity,
Or at least by her duty to respond in kind.   230
For when reason won't work, haranguing the girl
Will only succeed in hardening her mind.
In fact, the best thing is often to leave
Such people alone to fight with their fool-
ishness all by themselves. Since one mistake   235
Leads to another, as a general rule
They will follow their folly as far as they can,
And be forced to give in by the end of the day.
When someone's wandering in the dark
And thinks he may have lost his way,   240
To help him see that he took a wrong turn,
A stumble is just as good as a light.
Well, once I had concluded my
Research, and found out that her spite
Was rooted in a general distaste,   245
Not some offensiveness in me,
My duty here became quite clear:
Why should I be as stubborn as she?
And the more I pondered, the more I felt
That this rather ethereal vision   250
Of hers was something hardly worth
My pains, and more worth my derision.
Well, I guess I needed to be taught
How abject, how incredibly base
My human nature could finally get—   255
That a girl with such a lovely face,
With all of her airs of self-possession,
Could seem at first to be quite vapid,
But once I felt her full disdain,
My feelings underwent a rapid   260
Reversal, and what before seemed common
Became exotic in my eyes.
Oh, the perverseness of desire!
Even when greed itself espies

A greater value in the thing nearby   265
Than in the thing beyond the seas,
The simple fact of absence alone
Makes fond our foolish fantasies,
Gives value to things beyond our reach
And we only prize the impossible dream.   270
So every time I would view her face,
More and more beautiful would she seem.
And so there sprang up within my breast
This sudden, swift, surprising flame,
That my heart, astonished to see the blaze,   275
Rushed back to discover whence it came,
Only to find there, silent and cool
The snow of her disdain, the ic-
y spark that first ignited the fire.
A warning that man should always think twice!   280
Up till then I'd been fairly sure
That the ashes were cold, and there was no
Life left in the fire of love.
How was I tricked into thinking so!
If love can start a fire with snow,   285
What can it do with a pile of ash?
Flung to the ground by my own affections,
I gave my panting heart a lash-
ing: "Treacherous heart! what are you doing?
What are you doing? Rebel desire!   290
The girl didn't move a muscle to thank you,
How can disdain set you on fire?
You saw she wasn't the least impressed,
That ingrate has no right to my heart!
Do you find her beauty somehow enhanced   295
By the harshness that shines through her every part?
Why should disdain make something seem lovely
That without disdain was merely cool?
Isn't an insult truly an injury?
Shouldn't you bristle when someone is cruel?   300
If she couldn't attract you as a friend,
How can she as an enemy?

When beauty stoops to cruelty
Doesn't it lose its divinity?
How can something seem noble to me 305
Which in her is utter infamy?
Don't you despise all tyranny?
Then why seek to impose a tyrant on me?
What is this thing? Is it really love?
Is beauty perhaps a tyrant then? 310
No, it can't be love! It's a fraud!
No! May it never be said of men,
That sour women can win their souls
Without the touch of something sweet!
Then what is this thing? Isn't it burning? 315
Oh yes! I feel too well the heat!
Oh no, what frost ever fueled a flame?
Oh yes, is not my breast on fire?
It is not so, it cannot be!
Oh no, it would make truth a liar! 320
What is it then? It is desire!
For what? Is it my death I need?
I cannot love myself so ill!
What is it then? All right, it's greed,
For riches kept beyond my reach! 325
That cannot be, my heart has never
Been covetous. Is it madness then?
No. All right then, soul. Whatever
Can it be? A mind debased and low?
No, there's a kind of sovereignty 330
In human natures touched like ours,
A sense of refined supremacy
Which loves, which craves to be admired
For its native superiority.
And when it finds a heart too proud 335
To yield to its gallantry,
The shock and hurt of this disdain
Can set it afire, and at the stake
Can make it burn with a kind of passion,
Which forces the inflamed heart to make 340

A vow to conquer impossible things;
And wearied at last my the strength of the fire,
This heart surrenders to a kind of feeling,
A feeling more of shame than desire,
And fools itself into thinking it's love,   345
Because of its longings and heartfelt sighs;
But these feelings are nothing more
Than equivocations and outright lies."
This was the lecture my reason gave.
But my will was too debased to be   350
Convinced; it tore my reason and
Plucked all my courage away from me.
So whether it's love or infatuation,
Fire or snow, ashes or flame,
I am ablaze, and commit myself   355
To avenge my honor in the name
Of love—farewell the tranquil mind,
And the sweet peace of my liberty.
Here stand I, bereft of hope,
Looking for no remedy,   360
Ready to suffer without a word,
Feeding myself to the hungry jaws
Of pain like a willing sacrifice.
My pain begets more pain because
What drives me now is more than desire;   365
The lightning flash that fires me
To pursue this cause—however high—
Is its very irrationality.
And this is why my blinded will
Rushes headlong to bear the pain,   370
Subjecting itself to the tyranny
Of the spite and cruelty of her disdain.
And if I die, it is not for love,
But at finding myself in this shameful plight:
That a woman can attract me, not by her beauty   375
But by treating me with disdain and spite.
POLILLA:
A fine speech, sir, and I hung on every word,

And I'm not the least surprised by what you say.
The fact is, sir, the thing that you describe
Is something that happens every day.   380
Listen, sir, I grew up in a house,
Where everyone was cultivating
Grapes. While they were on the ground,
I never found them fascinating.
But later on, when they were hung up   385
In the kitchen for the long winter season,
At the sight of these dripping clusters of juicy
Pink grapes—I completely lost my reason.
I had to have them. And once climbing
Up on a chair to seize 'em and bite 'em   390
I fell and shattered all of my ribs.
Your case exactly, item for item.
It's natural, sir, it's the way things are.
CARLOS:
But, Moth, that's no relief to me,
When what is natural is so unfair!   395
POLILLA:
Then tell me, sir, this girl, does she
Give anyone else her favor?
CARLOS:
                No.
POLILLA:
Do any others try to win it?
CARLOS:
They're falling over themselves to get it.
POLILLA:
Oh, then she's sure to give in any minute,   400
I'll wager.
CARLOS:
          Why do you say that?
POLILLA:
Precisely because she's so disdainful.
CARLOS:
But how can that be?
POLILLA:
             I'll give you an example;

And I'll try not to make it too painful:
You know how boys all love to eat 405
Figs? And you know there's always this one
At the very top of the tree? And they all
Throw stones at it? And it hangs on,
And on, under this barrage of stones,
And then when it's ripe, it falls to the ground? 410
Now compare this to your situation.
She's up in the air, all firm and round,
And you throw all your stones at her,
And they all throw their stones as well,
And she'll hang on for a while, and then 415
One of these stones, only time will tell,
Will bring her down, when she's good and ripe,
And she's gonna be juicier than a fig;
But you gotta watch closely when she falls,
'Cause catching her is what counts big— 420
And she's gonna fall, sure as God made grapes.

CARLOS:
Look, here comes the count her father.

POLILLA:
And he's not alone. The Prince of Bearne
Is at his side, as well as the other
One, Gastón, the Count of Fox. 425

CARLOS:
None of them knows a thing about this,
About the fire that's in my heart,
My silence has muffled the ugly hiss
Of the poisonous serpent coiled in my breast.

POLILLA:
Now that's what I call bravery; 430
To feel so deeply and hold your tongue!
Well, I'm impressed. O, mercy me!
D'you know why a lover is often called blind?

CARLOS:
Because he doesn't use eyes to see.

POLILLA:
Nope.

CARLOS:
            Then why?
POLILLA:
                        Because you find   435
Blind beggars and lovers are two of a kind.
CARLOS:
How so?
POLILLA:
            By singing the same sad song
To every poor soul that comes along.
(Enter the Count of Barcelona, the Prince of Bearne, and Don Gastón, the
Count of Fox.)
COUNT:
 Princes, I know exactly how you feel.
If you think about it, I'm suffering more than you.   440
I've simply got no way to heal
The girl, as long as she's determined to
Continue being perverse and blind.
And every day she gets much worse, I find.
 The fact that I'm her father she ignores,   445
I've worn out every argument I had.
Whenever I try to talk of love, she roars
Herself into a frenzy. She's quite mad.
And to conclude she won't be wooed or wedded;
She'd rather die than let herself be bedded.   450
GASTÓN:
 Sir, may a humble hearer speak his part?
The real point, I take it, of your fine oration
Is that only time or reason can change her heart,
In that, I see no cause for desperation.
COUNT:
My dear Count Fox, all that may be quite true,   455
But I wouldn't want the job you have to do:
 Making the service of beauty your only mission,
Without the least encouragement from her.
BEARNE:
Dear sir, with your most kind permission,
It's just a silly whim, it won't endure.   460

And while it won't be easy to bend her will,
Time flies, my lord, and we are standing still.
 I left Bearne only for this intent;
Constant I am, and failing this would be
A greater disgrace than fancy can invent   465
Upon the poorest wretch of inconstancy,
A blot upon the very face of beauty,
And a blow to the heart of love's own sacred duty.
CARLOS:
 The Prince, dear sir, has answered you aright,
As a gallant, lovelorn gentleman should do,   470
For me, I'm a kind of reckless, wandering knight,
Who comes to jousts he was never invited to,
And wooing's not a skill I'm proficient in,
Yet failing to try would be a greater sin.
COUNT:
 All I can see, dear princes, is your insistence   475
On being stubborn. These are unmistakable signs
She's giving of superior resistance.
If all your feasts, your jousts, your grand designs,
Have failed to budge her an inch, what new invention
Can you dream up, to get the girl's attention?   480
POLILLA:
 Sir, even a fool can sometimes find a trick
That reason approves of. If you will permit,
I will prescribe a medicine for this sick-
ness, to turn those eyes of hers (that couldn't admit
The sight of them before) into fountains tear-   485
fully gushing over any of these men here.
COUNT:
 Who has the medicine like that?
POLILLA:
                                    I do.
Throwing a thankless girl a joust, I'd say,
Is like showing a seasick man a pot of stew.
So here's my cure, apply it without delay.   490
Take the Princess and lock her in one of those towers,
And keep her away from food for ninety-six hours.

And then let all the gentlemen form a line
And march beneath her window, carrying plates;
The first can carry six chickens; the next, some wine;   495
The third can carry a pie of raisins and dates,
And the devil can carry my soul to hell, if the little
Girl doesn't leap right out and land in the middle.
CARLOS:
 Are you crazy? Shut up, you fool!
POLILLA:

                                    What's craz-
y? Apply the medicine, sir—give it a try!   500
Starve her beauty for just four little days,
And you'll see, the girl will cast a loving eye
On the man who goes out for a walk in his Sunday best
With strips of bacon stapled to his vest.
BEARNE:
 For myself I have but this request, dear sir—   505
I'm sure it's the same as Don Gastón's intent—
We've never been given a chance to speak to her
Directly. Will you give us your consent
To see if sense and speech can change her mind?
COUNT:
I will, but I warn you, she's always declined.   510
 You try to think of something bold or endearing
Enough to shake her self-control; I'll go
And try to convince her to give you two a hearing.
I'm doing all I can, as you well know,
To help you win your just and worthy suit,   515
And get myself a princely heir to boot.
(Exit Count.)
BEARNE:
 Princes, it's little credit to the noble strain
Of our heroical bloods, to let a strong-
willed beauty treat us with such cool disdain.
Let's talk to her together.
CARLOS:

                              I'll go along   520
With you on this, but not at love's behest.

'Tis not the grail of love I seek in my quest.

GASTÓN:
Well, then, if you've outflown blind Cupid's wings,
What means would you suggest to bend her will?
The unbiased eye has the clearest view of things.   525

CARLOS:
I do know one, but silence keeps me still,
Because if I shared this other way with you.
One or the other would want to try it, too.

BEARNE:
You're very wise.

GASTÓN:
                    Bearne, let's go conspire;
We'll plot more feasts, more finery, more games.   530

BEARNE:
To crack the ice of her disdain with fire.

GASTÓN:
And melt her frosty coolness in our flames.

CARLOS:
I'll help with that.

BEARNE:
                    Then on to triumph glorious!

(Exeunt Gastón and Bearne.)

CARLOS:
And fortune make the luckiest man victorious!

POLILLA:
Excuse me, sir, did I hear you maintain   535
You weren't in love?

CARLOS:
                    I have another road to take,
To conquer such extraordinary disdain;
Come on, boy, you and I have plans to make
About how you can help me.

POLILLA:
                    Help you? Of course.

CARLOS:
Can you get inside?

POLILLA:
                    I could build a Trojan horse.   540

CARLOS:
 Can you really get in?
POLILLA:

                 To have a look aroun'?
It's me, sir, Moth! What are you thinking of?
I can chew a hole in the thickest gown!
CARLOS:
Then let me propose a toast! Here's to my love!
Come on—if that's the plot, I know my part;   545
I can nibble the rest of the way—into her heart.
(Exeunt Carlos and Polilla.)
(Enter the Musicians, Diana, Cintia, Laura, and the Ladies.)
MUSICIANS: *(Singing)*
 The lovely Daphne, fleeing
Apollo, mocked his fidelity.
He shot his bolt at seeing her fly,
But she was saved by a laurel tree.   550
DIANA:
 Ay me, that sounds so beautiful—
This noble disdain they're singing of!
What woman would ever want to love!
What heart would be so dutiful!
CINTIA: *(Aside)*
 What kind of wit would look at love   555
And think it was against the law;
Or think it could correct a flaw
That Nature itself is guilty of!
DIANA:
 More, more of your harmony!
Go on, the author of this song   560
Clearly sees how false and wrong
Is the little love-god's tyranny.
MUSICIANS: *(Singing)*
 There's little room or none at all,
'Twixt love and gratitude;
To insure the triumph of her disdain.   565
A lady sometimes must be rude.

DIANA:

 Well said! Love's such a little child;
And gratitude, however pure,
Is always a step, slow but sure,
Down the path that leads to being beguiled.   570
 For gratitude is a kind of reward
One pays to love by being nice,
And any woman who pays that price
Shows that she yearns to be adored.
 A thankful woman has all but proved   575
She likes to be loved. And has anyone seen
Any real difference between
Loving, and loving to be loved?

CINTIA:

 To be thankful, Diana, and not to be rude
Is a noble and courtly duty.   580
And it's unfair to a gracious beauty
To say that her graciousness makes her lewd.
 When we give thanks, we do so in the name
Of reason, which prompts us to it.
When we seek love, the will makes us do it.   585
The two causes are not the same.
 Then if there is such separation,
Both of cause and of intent,
Surely the reason may rightly consent,
Without the will's cooperation.   590

DIANA:

 One can appreciate a thing, I confess,
That one is not enamored of.
For the will is indeed the cause of love
And reason the cause of thankfulness.
 I'm not saying that a lady *has* to fall   595
In love because she's gracious, my dear;
It's just that to me such women appear
To be looking for a tumble, that's all.
 And frankly anyone that unaware
Is either unseeing or unafraid   600
Of the risk she takes. No prudent maid

Would ever set her foot in that snare.
CINTIA:
 Ingratitude to one and all
Is criminal discourtesy.
DIANA:
But overfond civility   605
Goeth before a fall.
CINTIA:
 It's a crime I won't permit.
DIANA:
It's a risk I will not take.
CINTIA:
But is it then all right to break
A law, to avoid some loss that it   610
 Might bring?
DIANA:
                    Yes, as long as you feel
There's a possible risk.
CINTIA:
                    But then the loss
Would be less, since the risk is only poss-
ible, when the crime itself is real.
DIANA:
 No, it's a greater sin to be guilty of   615
Loving than failing in gratitude.
CINTIA:
But wouldn't it be best, if you could,
To dispense the thanks but spare the love?
DIANA:
 No, since love is always the result.
CINTIA:
But can't you stop at appreciation?   620
DIANA:
If you don't resist the first temptation
Resisting the rest will be difficult.
CINTIA:
 But isn't it better, after all,
To be a model of courtesy

And prove as well one's constancy, 625
By giving the thanks but avoiding the fall?
DIANA:
 No, that gives love an opening;
And it's hard enough to defeat love
When it's kept out, but to beat love
When it's in, is a very different thing. 630
CINTIA:
 Then if it's true what you're speaking of,
It's a chance worth taking, it seems to me.
And rather than sin against courtesy,
I'd gladly risk falling in love.
DIANA:
 How dare you talk so recklessly 635
Or so boldly! Love! What is that?
You must have forgotten where you're at!
You are in front of me!
 Love! how can you even think such a thing!
Love, in the same room with me? 640
No, no, this cannot be!
Laura, please, go on, sing.
MUSICIANS: *(Singing)*
Don't trust in Love's caresses,
Though he looks like a babe on the wing;
He may have the face of a little child 645
But he commands like a king.
(Polilla enters, dressed as a doctor.)
POLILLA:
 (Here's hoping my entrance will produce
A little spark.)
DIANA:
                    Who can this be?
POLILLA:
Ego.
DIANA:
                Who's that?
POLILLA:
                        Mihi, vel mi!

Ego sum scholasticus,
    Pauper et enamoratus.   650
DIANA:
Enamoratus means 'in love'—
Don't come in here, what are you thinking of?
POLILLA:
No, no, miss, I said *examinatus.*
DIANA:
 Examined? For what?
POLILLA:
                          For love most cruel.   655
And passing the test, earned my degree
As *Doctor Amoris,* which promoted me,
From being a failure to being a fool.
DIANA:
 Where do you come from?
POLILLA:
                              I come from…a place.
DIANA:
That's true.
POLILLA:
                    Aha! But that in   660
Translation is *loco* in Latin.
DIANA:
I can see that.
POLILLA:
                    Then gallop apace!
DIANA:
 Why have you come?
POLILLA:
                          I heard of the fame
Of your ladyship, with this addition—
That you had a most rare disposition.   665
DIANA:
And where did you hear of my name?
POLILLA:
 In Acapulco.

DIANA:

Where's that, if you please?

POLILLA:

'Bout half a mile from Viñaroz.
I had a craving to diagnose
And cure this terrible itching disease   670
 You get from a bout of love. I would
Have to come and see you here
And learn, God willing, from you the cure.
So I left Havana as fast as I could,
 To get to Barcelona.   675
I ran my horses nearly dead—

DIANA:

You *rode* from Havana, you said?

POLILLA:

Yes, and dismounted at Tarragona,
 Whence have I hastened here to be
With you; on foot did I outrace   680
The sun from the sky, to see your face.

DIANA:

And what exactly do you see in me?

POLILLA:

 A power that leaves me nearly bereft
Of my senses! Love can command
No sharper arrow than your right hand—   685
Unless of course, you use your left.

DIANA:

 You're in a good humor!

POLILLA:

                    I see—
You like my conversation?

DIANA:

Yes.

POLILLA:

              Then the barest occupation
Is all I'd need to satisfy me.   690

DIANA:

 I'll give you one.

POLILLA:
                    Let me kiss—no! that's
Wrong! Did I say kiss? No kiss!
DIANA:
Why not?
POLILLA:
            It's not just a kiss! What it is,
Is bait for love's trap, like cheese for rats.
DIANA:
 I will employ you.
POLILLA:
                    God is merc-   695
iful. Make it a decent position.
DIANA:
You mean you're not a physician?
POLILLA:
I'm still studying. I could be a nurse.
DIANA:
 And this lovesickness, this fatal
Disease, how would you cure it?
POLILLA:
                         I have   700
For the French disease, a silvery salve.
DIANA:
And it works?
POLILLA:
            Silver's a potent metal.
DIANA:
 Are you ill now?
POLILLA:
                Of a mortal infection—
Named "love." Love, said Averroës
Is not so much a disease   705
As a hernia. He said affection
 Grips the guts and causes cruc-
ifying pain. Love is a crime—
Treason, tyranny—only by time
Is it cured, and a diet of crackers and juice.   710

Love, madam, is all confusion,
All tossing and turning, the torments of hell,
And love is flattery as well,
And charms the beard off a Carthusian.
Love sweet-talks a women affectionately,   715
Calls her sugar and honey and pet,
But a lady who buys his line doesn't get
A lifetime guarantee.

DIANA:
I suppose I could give you a job as
My jester—it's all I have   720
Open right now.

POLILLA:
                    It's all I crave!
It's why I came from Casabas!

DIANA:
Casabas?

POLILLA:
            My birthplace, Fam-
ous little roadside stop,
Known for its annual crop   725
Of melons. Hence the name.

DIANA:
And what is yours?

POLILLA:
                    It's Satin, ma'am.

DIANA:
Well, Satin. Your coming here
Pleases me greatly.

POLILLA:
                    Lady dear,
I live to serve. That's who I am.   730
(So now I've found a way to get in.
What a world we live in today
Where the princely man may lose his way,
And the lowly clown may win!
Well, if Carlos can't win the rest   735
Of her heart, he's a fool—now that his moth

Has already chewed a hole in the cloth
That covers the lady's breast.)
LAURA:
 Here comes your father, madam, and he's got
The princes with him. They're coming in, too!   740
DIANA:
The princes are with him? What do you mean?
Good heavens, what is he trying to do?
If he's going to insist again that I
Get married, I swear I'd sooner slit
My throat with a butcher knife.   745
CINTIA:
Are men so bad? I wonder what it
Can be she finds so abhorrent? Laura,
Tell me, how can she not delight
In the dashing and daring Count of Urgel?
LAURA:
I think the girl's a hermaphrodite!   750
CINTIA:
He's nearly stolen my eyes from me!
LAURA:
Well, frankly, my nose has always been
Partial to satin handkerchiefs;
I like the feel of it on my skin.
(Enter the Count, and the three Princes.)
COUNT:
Princes, please, come in with me.   755
CARLOS:
(Those eyes—they steal away my heart!
I don't think I've got the courage now
To keep on playing my part.
She's lovelier than she was before!)
DIANA:
Good heavens! What could this be?   760
COUNT:
Daughter! Diana!
DIANA:
                Sir?

COUNT:
I'm fully aware of your delicacy,
As well as the debt I owe these princes
For the festive shows they've offered you;
They've also made it clear to me,   765
How much your keeping yourself from view
Has hurt their feelings, my dear, and they—
DIANA:
I beg you, sir, let me be heard,
Before you go any further with this,
Before you give these men your word   770
To perform an act by which your good
And my desires are both overthrown.
First of all, let me say, that with you
I have no will of my own,
Nor ever could; to do your will   775
Is all the freedom I've ever known.
Second, about my marrying:
Sir, marrying me off would be like tak-
ing my neck and putting it in a noose,
And my heart in the mouth of a snake.   780
Marrying and dying are the same to me;
But I'd sooner die than disobey
Your command. Well, that's settled.
Now, what did you want to say?
COUNT:
Daughter, you've got me completely wrong.   785
I never intended to force you to marry;
I'm only trying to discharge my debt
To these gentlemen for the very
Festive shows they put on for you,
The best of which has been their display   790
Of courtesy, which surely deserves
A reward—which if you won't pay
With your favor, then I must with my thanks.
And though you are in no way bound
To accept their offers, you ought to respect   795
Them for my sake, lest the people around

Suspect some grievous fault of mine
In hospitality, instead
Of this strange aversion which you seem
To have against your being wed.   800
And finally, I've never considered this
A refusal to obey some commandment of
Mine, because I never ordered you
To do it. No, it's just that the love
I have for you, moves me to want   805
To please you, and since when you please
Yourself, you can neither disobey
Me, nor offer an insult to these
Fine gentlemen, why not tell them
The secret reasons for this life you've select-   810
ed, which seems to agree so well with you,
And surely deserves all my respect.
(And the Count leaves.)
DIANA:
Well, sirs, if that's all you want from me,
Then listen, and I'll be glad to explain.
GASTÓN:
That's the only reason we are here.   815
BEARNE:
Since it strikes us so odd that you'd abstain
From marriage, there's little cause for you
To wonder why we wonder why.
CARLOS:
And as for me, although I've come
To learn your reasons, it's not that I   820
Find anything to wonder at; it's just
I have a scientific mind.
DIANA:
Then listen and I'll explain it all.
POLILLA:
(My God, this oughta be good—to find
A reason strong enough to explain   825
Her case. Some story this'll be—
To give them a reason for being insane!)

DIANA:
I remember the day it came to me—
Ever since the first rays of reason
Began to shine on me, and my sense   830
Of understanding dawned, and I
Began to use my intelligence,
I dedicated my life to the task
Of reading all that could be read
Of history, where time itself   835
Gives lessons for the days ahead
With examples drawn from the past.
And oh! what ruin, what devastation,
What tragedies, and what confusions,
To every people in every nation,   840
From the humblest to the highest—
And all these griefs were born of love!
No matter what the wise men knew,
No matter how brightly the genius of
Philosophy lit men's moral lives,   845
They wasted their light, trying to prevent
In every age that went before,
The blindness, error, violent
Behavior, madness, tyranny
Of the God of lies, who uses such fair   850
Words of affection to enter the heart
And plant a volcano there.
What lover ever told his tale
To the world, that was not a litany
Of tears and sighs and deep laments,   855
Of wretchedness and misery,
Of moans and groans and sad complaints,
Filling all the air around
With the pitiful song of grief and loss,
And echoing back the bitter sound?   860
And even when love was kind and let
A lover find a loving mate,
How often were they torn apart,
By the hand of God or the curse of fate!

So then, since anyone who weds 865
Is bound to love by oath and word,
How could you ever think to marry
Once you knew the risk you incurred?
And a loveless marriage would be a cause
Without an effect. Unless you have 870
Complete submission to the master's will,
Why would you make yourself his slave?
Could you find a prison for your heart
More wretched and more dire
Than to surrender your will to a man 875
Who's not the object of your desire?
To love and obey is the marriage vow,
An impossible coexistence
When you only obey in outward things,
With an inwardly resistance. 880
So loving or loveless, either way,
I've concluded never to wed;
Loving because it's dangerous,
And loveless because I rather be dead.

BEARNE:

With your permission, let me be 885
The first to answer this proposition.

GASTÓN:

It's quite all right with me.

CARLOS:

Whatever I said would be repetition.
My own opinion is exactly the same
As Lady Diana's position. 890

BEARNE:

Deception's subtlest strategy
In the war against intelligence
Is ever to come wearing the clothes
Of seemingly rational arguments.
But Love has arguments of its own 895
To counter those; and they are not
As weak as faulty logic likes
To think they are. But enough of thought!

Experience can make the case
Far better than mere intellect,   900
Since it alone can marshal proofs
Drawn directly from effect.
And if you don't put yourself to the test,
You make a mistake that can't be resolved,
Since there's no way to gain experience   905
If you've sworn never to get involved.
You're going against the rational order
Of things, and you're making war
With all the power of your reason
Against the strength of natural law.   910
Don't close your lovely ears to the truths
We're trying to tell you about;
Because if it's reasonable not to love,
There's no risk to reason in hearing us out.
But if it's not, then time will force   915
Your total capitulation;
And time's triumphant victory
Will be your public humiliation.
You be the champion of disdain,
We'll be the challenging knights,   920
You make your cause the defense of reason,
And meet us in our tournament fights.
Convene your academy of spite
In the very lists of our gallantry,
Where the only argument we have   925
Is the honor of our chivalry.
We'll see then which of us is right,
For we dedicate ourselves alone
To the task of winning you to love
Or seeing our challenges overthrown.   930
DIANA:
In order then that you may see
That this opinion of mine is the one
True, clear-eyed daughter of sober sense,
And yours is error's only son,
I'll place my beauty on the line;   935

Hold you then your tournament,
And use whatever ways and means
That Love can find or wit invent.
From this time on I'll give myself
To receive your tilts and gallantry   940
With open ear and open eye,
To prove the impossibility
Of my ever falling in love,
And that this disdain which I've professed,
In practice as well as in theory,   945
Is the natural offspring of my breast.

GASTÓN:
Then if we must, from this day on,
Use chivalry as our campaign,
Let's all begin our bold foray
Against our foes, scorn and disdain.   950
Princes, the challenge has been made
Between love and reason. Be diligent!
Let each man choose his favorite means
To pursue the argument.
Come let us go, that we may see   955
Whose choice is most expedient.
(He goes out.)

BEARNE:
I go at once to choose out mine,
And, Lady, I hope it may befall
That you may prove against yourself
The sharpest argument of all.   960
(And he goes out.)

CARLOS:
And I, milady, will go as well,
Duty bound—as these princes went—
To join in the festivities—
But not, I swear, with their intent.

DIANA:
Then why?

CARLOS:
             Because I too believe   965

In the very opinion that you hold.
Yet your opinion is your own,
And mine is, well, rather more bold.
DIANA:
How so? In what way bolder?
CARLOS:
Lady,

Not only will I never fall 970
In love, I won't be loved as well.
DIANA:
What risk in being loved?
CARLOS:
None at all—

No risk, but a terrible sin.
There can be no risk, because my breast
Is like a battlement secure 975
At every moment against the best
Assault of love. If heaven itself
Assembled a lady from the fairest part
Of every beauty, and she adored me,
She'd find no sympathy in my heart. 980
But it would be a sin, because I know
That I could not love her back, you see;
And to be beloved and not to respond
Is surely a sin against courtesy.
And thus it is, that I will not love, 985
Nor have another in love with me.
Because I hate to be unkind,
As I know that I would have to be.
DIANA:
But still you wish to join the feasts
Without any love for me? Is that true? 990
CARLOS:
Of course.
DIANA:
But why?

CARLOS:
To fulfill the debt

Of veneration I owe to you.

DIANA:
But isn't that love?

CARLOS:
                    Love? Oh, No!
Milady, it's nothing but respect.

POLILLA:
(Body of Christ, what a beautiful cut!   995
What a clean incision! Now just select
Some vinegar, and marinate,
And you'll see before the sun goes down
She'll be pickled and ready to eat.)

DIANA: *(Aside to Cinta)*
Cintia, did you hear this clown?   1000
He's so absurd he's almost funny.

CINTIA: *(Aside to Diana)*
He's arrogant.

DIANA:
                    What a joke it would be,
To make that fool fall in love!

CINTIA:
But there's a certain risk I see.

DIANA:
What risk?

CINTIA:
            Of falling in love yourself,   1005
If you don't manage the thing just right.

DIANA:
Then you're a bigger fool than he!
Whatever makes you think that I might?
If all their fawning has left me cold,
What chance has his pride of warming me?   1010

CINTIA:
Ma'am, it was just an observation.

DIANA:
That's why crushing his vanity
Becomes a moral obligation.

CINTIA: *(Aside)*
I rather like this turn of events.
DIANA:
Sir—fire your blaze of chivalry   1015
And I will reward your beneficence
With a greater debt of gratitude
Than love could ever bind me to.
CARLOS:
Then you're prepared to treat me kindly?
DIANA:
Because there can't be a risk with you.   1020
CARLOS:
Then I go, my lady, to oblige you the more.
DIANA:
And I'll have thanks to match your best.
CARLOS:
Only beware: don't fall in love.
For then I'll be forced to abandon the quest.
DIANA:
My lord, I don't even give it a thought.   1025
CARLOS:
Then, lady, I rush to embrace my task!
DIANA:
Then go, my lord! Where is my Satin?
CARLOS: *(Aside to Polilla)*
Her what?
POLILLA: *(Aside to Carlos)*
          I'm a man of the cloth now; she's ask-
ing for me.
DIANA:
          Cintia, get ready to watch
Him grovel.
CINTIA:
          So you said before.   1030
But fate has a way of turning the tables.
(And frankly nothing would please me more.)
(Cintia goes out.)

DIANA:
But do you hear, sir?
CARLOS:

                What's your will?
DIANA:
What if time should change your decision?
CARLOS:
About what?
DIANA:

       About loving.
CARLOS:

               What then?   1035
DIANA:
You'd become an object of derision.
CARLOS:
And what if love gets a hold of you?
DIANA:
I'm not going to love.
CARLOS:

              I don't think you will.
DIANA:
Then why did you ask?
CARLOS:

             There's always a chance—
DIANA:
The chance is something less than nil.   1040
CARLOS:
But if it happens—
DIANA:

             It's not going to.
CARLOS:
Just wondering.
DIANA:

          I give you my word.
CARLOS:
That's all I desire.
DIANA:

         Then all is well.

You can rest assured.

CARLOS:
                    Go in peace with the Lord.

DIANA:
(Whatever the cost, I've got to teach   1045
This fool a lesson—I don't care how!)
(Diana goes out, with her ladies and musicians.)

POLILLA:
You're leading her quite a merry dance!

CARLOS:
I'm dying, Moth, I've overstayed
My welcome in the world, I've sapped
My strength with this masquerade.   1050

POLILLA:
Come on, sir, on your feet at once.
You'll see—it's a nice little fire you've made.

CARLOS:
That's something—

POLILLA:
                    Come on, you see,
I got inside. I've already *been* in.

CARLOS:
But how'd you do it?

POLILLA:
                    With the 'Satin,' sir;   1055
I've made myself part of the household linen.
(They go out.)

Act Two
(Enter Carlos and Polilla.)

CARLOS:
 O Moth, my friend, I'm in distress,
And you bring relief. Come, give me the cure
For an aching heart.

POLILLA:

                   Whoa, calm down, sir,
If you please. I've got a lot to confess.   1060

CARLOS:
 Tell me all. My love and my fears
Are killing each other.

POLILLA:

                   I'm sorry, this
Is too close, sir; I don't want a kiss,
Just a couple of feet and both your ears.
 Well, first of all, the princes out there   1065
Are acting like total nincompoops.
They're throwing parties, and jumping through hoops,
And dashing their hopes beyond repair.
 They're heaping feast upon feast, and there's not
The slightest crack in her disdain,   1070
And all their games are played in vain,
She doesn't even give them a thought.
 They've wasted every penny they've spent,
Creating a debt she'll never repay.
They took the surest straightest way   1075
Not to get to her love. They went
 Right down the wrong street and out
Of her favor. They're positive proof
That the only road that leads under her roof
Is not direct but roundabout.   1080
 I'm certain of this one thing at least,
The mock disdain you aimed at her
Has luckily wounded her for sure—
She called for Last Rites and sent for a priest.
 Yes, she shared with my duplicity   1085

The secrets of that lovely breast,
And to yours truly the girl confessed,
As to a doctor of divinity.
 And the very first thing she always want-
ed to know was what she should do   1090
To defeat you. (Would you look at who
The lady chose for a confidante!)
 So I would give her a solemn bless-
ing and say, "If that's all you fear,
There's not a fitter means, my dear,   1095
Than your own loveliness.
 Just like a kiss in the game of croquet,
An occasional sweetness can be very winning;
A little touch and you send him spinning,
Then you turn around and smile and say,   1100
 'Gotcha!'" Frankly, she seems to me
So totally taken by your ruse
That I wouldn't be shocked if the lady woos
You first. And then it'll be
 Important, sir, for you to rehearse   1105
That stony face, that self-control,
However cruel, to keep your soul
As inviolate as a miser's purse.
 She's a dish you could burn your tongue on.
Don't be such a fool to assume   1110
That the lady's heart has a vacant room
For you, because of some sign she's hung on
 Her door with a hammer and nail.
When you're close enough to make it out,
You'll see exactly what it's all about,   1115
It says, "This house is not for sale!"

CARLOS:
 And what do I gain by this delay?

POLILLA:
The lady'll bite—I have no doubt.

CARLOS:
And how do you manage to figure out
That the lady will have to 'bite' as you say?   1120

POLILLA:
She'll 'bite' all right! Heavens above!
I give her ten days to keep up the pretense,
And if you maintain your diffidence,
By the eleventh she'll be madly in love.
 By the twelfth, she'll feel decidedly giddy.   1125
And by the thirteenth, it seems to me,
(And what an unlucky day that'll be!)
She'll go down on her knees and beg for your pity.
CARLOS:
 I have a feeling that you're right;
But it's my passion I'm terrified of;   1130
If she gives me a single glance of love,
I'll never be able to treat her with spite.
POLILLA:
 You're talking like a lovesick maid!
CARLOS:
But what can I do?
POLILLA:
                    Show her how chill-
y you are.
CARLOS:
                    When I'm frying on the grill?   1135
POLILLA:
So drink a lemonade!
CARLOS:
 I'd better double the guard I've set
On my heart.
POLILLA:
                    What's wrong with my memory!
The best parts of our history
Are the very ones I always forget!   1140
 You know what day it is today?
It's Carnival time!
CARLOS:
                    What if it is?
POLILLA:
But here in Barcelona, this

Gorgeous city has a different way
  Of celebrating. When they have a dance,
A lady and gentleman pair up for the day,
With no commitments either way; 1145
Here in the palace they do it by chance.
  Each lady selects a color to wear;
Each man picks one when he comes in the door, 1150
And the lady who's wearing that color comes for-
ward and the matching couple becomes a pair.
  She pledges to favor him all the day,
And he to stick to her side like a mag-
net, which gets pretty funny when some old hag 1155
Gets her hooks into some young *chevalier*.
  Well that's how it's done, and Diana's plan
Is to get herself paired up with you,
And I don't know how she's managed to,
But you're her partner for the pavan; 1160
  The thing's a *fait accompli!*
But here she comes! Quick! Hide!
She mustn't find us together inside,
Or she'll get suspicious of me.

CARLOS:
  See if you can persuade her disdain 1165
To flirt with me.

POLILLA:
              Yeah, sure.
Like a dose of icewater's the perfect cure.
I think the fever just hit your brain.
(Carlos moves out of sight; Diana, Cintia and Laura enter.)

DIANA:
  Cintia, I think I've found the best
Way to sweep my wooer off his feet: 1170
I simply have to be more sweet
To him. So honor my one request:
  Bring all your colored sashes to
The dance, as I will mine.
Then you each can have whichever fine 1175
Young gallant pleases you,

Because whatever color he
Selects, you're ready with the match-
ing sash you've wisely brought to catch
Him with. Just leave with me
The one picked by my Cavalier.   1180

CINTIA:
That would be a real coup—
To make him fall in love with you,
Can you do that?

DIANA:
                            Is Satin here?

POLILLA:
 Light of my life, sun of my skies!   1185

DIANA:
What's the news?

POLILLA:
                        I've managed to get
Quite friendly with Carlos.

DIANA:
                                I'm in your debt—
You're such a help.

POLILLA:
                            So while I advise
 Him to stay on course, below deck
I'll be spying for you.
            (Aside) Don't think it won't work,   1190
This plan of mine. I'll just ease off the cork
And open up this bottleneck.

DIANA:
 But tell me what you found out, I beg
You—am I getting under his skin?

POLILLA:
Oh, milady, it's tough to get in,   1195
His hide's as thick as a hard-boiled egg.
 But I know a little fencing trick—
We can stick him till he roars with shame.

DIANA:
You'll have to guide my aim.

POLILLA: *(Aside)*
Poor thing, it's you you're going to prick.   1200
DIANA:
 I've got a thousand crowns you can have
If you can conquer his disdain.
POLILLA:
Oh, I can do it. For that kind of pain,
I've got a very special salve.
 But once you've got him all mushy and tender,   1205
How do you plan to use him?
DIANA:
How? I'll crush him, refuse him, abuse him,
I'll force him to see he has to surrender
 All his dear tranquility
To my eyes as a loving sacrifice.   1210
CARLOS:
(What a fire of love burns in those eyes!)
POLILLA:
(A double cross is a joy to see!)
 That's not as good as what *I'm* thinking of;
What would you say, once he's mortified,
To taking pity on his miserable hide?   1215
DIANA:
Pity? What do you mean?
POLILLA:
                        Well—love.
DIANA:
 Love? What do you mean?
POLILLA:
                        Well, not real-
ly full-blown love, you know, it's more
Like a taste of love; after all, an *hors
D'oeuvre's* not the same as a five-course meal.   1220
DIANA:
 Love? Is that what you're talking of?
Surrendering myself to him—what for?
I could see that man at death's door,
And even that wouldn't move me to love.

CARLOS: *(Aside to Polilla)*
Was there ever a woman so rare, so bold!   1225
She's cruelty itself!
POLILLA: *(Aside to Carlos)*
                  Just let
Me work. She'll not only see your bet,
But (sure as God lives!) she'll raise and fold.
CARLOS: *(Aside)*
 My soul's on fire, I'm telling you!
I'm going!
POLILLA:
             He's coming.
DIANA:
                  On with the show.   1230
POLILLA:
(What a terrible time she's picked to go
Public. Poor thing, if only she knew!)
DIANA:
 Cintia, warn us when it's time
To go to the dance.
CINTIA:
                I've taken care
That someone will keep us aware   1235
Of that.
CARLOS:
        And behold, milady, I'm
The first to arrive. It was the least
I could do, to fulfill my obligation.
DIANA:
But if you're so free from infatuation,
Why be so punctual at our feast?   1240
CARLOS:
 By keeping my heart from adoration,
Free from the worries and cares of love,
I give my soul the liberty of
Fulfilling its solemn obligation.
POLILLA: *(to Diana)*
 Toss him a little crumb of kind-   1245

ness to see if it interests him at all.

DIANA: *(to Polilla)*
That's what I'm doing.

POLILLA: *(Aside)*
                    This is what I call:
Teaching the girl to spit in the wind.

DIANA:
 Your presence here obliges me
The more, because you come without love.   1250

CARLOS:
But even without this evidence of
Your kindness, I would gladly be
 Your slave if you commanded. It's a debt
My presence here is bound to pay.

DIANA: *(to Polilla)*
Kindness adds less heat than you say.   1255

POLILLA: *(to Diana)*
The kindling's still a little wet.

DIANA:
 Then is any kindness which I show
Not worthy of your estimation?

CARLOS:
It is a kindness that with veneration
I'd repay, but not with love—oh, no.   1260

POLILLA: *(Aside)*
 Don't even pay her that, you lout!

CARLOS:
What can I do? When a lady is sweet—
Or pretends to be—it cools my heat.

POLILLA: *(Aside)*
Forget the sweets, just spit 'em out.

DIANA:
 What?

POLILLA:
            I said, when the lady speaks   1265
So nicely, he should be grateful to her.

DIANA:
You're right.

POLILLA: *(Aside)*

        And this is called, dear sir,
Talking with tongue in both your cheeks.

DIANA:

If the day ever came when I was inclined
To love, you'd be the man for me.   1270

CARLOS:

But why?

DIANA:

        There's a secret sympathy
Between the two of us, I find.
The fact that you share my dedication,
Means that we're one—spiritually.
If my will would permit it, you would be   1275
The natural object of my inclination.

CARLOS:

That would be a mistake.

DIANA:

        No, it wouldn't.
You're an ideal suitor.

CARLOS:

        No, that's not true.

DIANA:

Why not?

CARLOS:

      Because I promise you,
I wouldn't respond. I simply couldn't.   1280

DIANA:

Oh, surely, sir, of course you would.
If a woman like me fell in love with you,
You'd have to respond.

CARLOS:

        No.

DIANA:

          Is that true?

CARLOS:

I wouldn't deceive you if I could.

POLILLA: *(Aside)*

Courage, master, have no fear!   1285

Hit her again on the other cheek!
If you can't nail her when she's weak,
You can nail some horns on me—right here.
DIANA: *(Aside to Polilla)*
 I know I shouldn't be angry, but
Have you ever seen such arrogance?   1290
POLILLA: *(Aside to Diana)*
God's breath—sheer impudence!
DIANA: *(Aside to Polilla)*
You agree?
POLILLA: *(Aside to Diana)*
                    The man's a pig!
DIANA: *(Aside to Polilla)*
                                        Then what
Should I do?
POLILLA: *(Aside to Diana)*
                    Lead him down the prim-
rose path, then roast him through and through
With a blast of disdain.
DIANA: *(Aside to Polilla)*
                                    You're right, it's true!   1295
That's the best revenge I could have on him!
(to Carlos)
 I though you a man of intellect.
CARLOS:
Have I behaved unreasonably?
DIANA:
You just keep on insulting me.
CARLOS:
But I've done nothing in disrespect.   1300
 That you may see the error of
Anyone in the world who says
That loving is a form of praise,
Let me tell you the truth about love.
 To love, milady, is to have a breast   1305
In a constant state of inflammation,
Is to have a yearning heart obsessed
With seeing the cause of all this passion,

And this is love's glory, at its best.
The eyes, in greedy appreciation   1310
For anything they see, pass on
To the loving imagination,
The images they feed upon,
And this is what causes the inflammation
Of the heart, whose burning fever tries   1315
To quench imagination's thirst
With more of beauty, but as the eyes
Do gorge themselves, even to burst-
ing, still does the temperature rise.
This fever's fatal, and he that will   1320
For love return love back again,
Knowingly serves the lover ill,
Giving no remedy but pain
And making the sickness stronger still.
When a man is loved, it follows that he   1325
Is not required to return the love,
When doing so's an injury.
And nothing the lover does should move
The beloved to respond. You see,
The lover whose love is the purest strain   1330
Of passion, wants nothing less
Than to ease his heart of its crushing pain,
With the mere sight of the loveliness
It worships. Sight alone can sustain
The loving heart; the joy of sight   1335
Is the goal that draws the lover to love.
Seeing is loving at its very height;
The joy of beholding the vision of
The beloved all by itself can incite
The lover to love. For proof of this,   1340
Look at the lover whose love's unreturned;
He lives for love, but the pleasure's all his;
He gives nothing to the woman who's spurned
Him. No, he takes—it's his own bliss
He's after. Look at the lovers who   1345
Are hated by those that they love,

Are they sorry for what they do
To them? No, all they're aware of
Is the pain *they're* going through.
 When lovers are met with cold disdain, 1350
And suffer and still come back for more,
If they continue in spite of pain,
They seek not the good of her they adore,
But only the pleasure they can gain.
 So love itself will ever be 1355
To be-all and end-all for all its does.
And responding to love, it's clear to me,
Is not a duty, it never was,
Neither for love, nor sympathy.
DIANA:
 But love is surely the combination 1360
Of two souls, exchanging their very
Beings in a transformation,
For which three things are necessary:
Volition, attraction, and gratification.
 And if the pleasure is clearly the 1365
Result of choice and inclination,
And if the choice is volunt'ry,
Isn't responding an obligation
If not for love, then courtesy?
CARLOS:
 But if your reason teaches you 1370
That lovers deserve a dignified
Response, why spurn them when they woo?
DIANA:
Because I'm the one who has to decide
What's the right thing for me to do.
CARLOS:
 But isn't that acting unreasonably? 1375
DIANA:
I don't need a reason for what I do.
If I choose to do it, it's right for me.
CARLOS:
Then I have the same reason as you,

For not responding courteously.
DIANA:
 But what would happen if you should find   1380
Your pride had fallen, what would you say?
CARLOS:
If as you say we are one in mind,
And mine is overthrown some day,
Then, lady, can yours be far behind?
(Music sounds.)
LAURA:
 Lady Diana, the trumpets call!   1385
Now is the hour to begin the ball.
Summon the suitors to the hall,
For this is the time of Carnival.
POLILLA:
All the princes ready stand.
DIANA: *(Aside to the ladies)*
Attention, ladies! as we've planned   1390
Keep all your colors near at hand.
POLILLA: *(Aside to Carlos)*
On guard, master—take command!
CARLOS: *(Aside to Polilla)*
Oh, Moth, I can't pretend—
It's killing me—my life's at an end!
POLILLA: *(Aside to Carlos)*
Be quiet! What's left of it you'll spend   1395
With her—she's the special of the day;
You'll be stuffing yourself on love, I'd say.
CARLOS: *(Aside to Polilla)*
They're coming, Moth, don't give us away.
(Enter the Princes, and the Musicians singing.)
MUSICIANS: *(Singing)*
 Gentles, come, come one and all,
Claim a lady for your prize,   1400
For this is the Feast of Carnival,
And Love wears a disguise.
 Fa-la-ra-la, fa-la-ra-la, etc.
BEARNE:
I come, Milady, full of doubt,

Born under an unlucky star,
Yet trusting that Fortune will help me out.

GASTÓN:
I have doubts, too—they are
The same; yet I know that Fate
Which gives me now the chance to choose,
Will still be true to my estate,
And take good care I may not lose.

DIANA:
Then sit you down, and every one
Select a color, and let him say,
As is our custom, before 'tis done,
The reason why he chose that way.
And she who bears the color of
His choice, let her come forth, and let
It be his duty to show her love,
And hers with grace to repay that debt.

MUSICIANS: *(Singing)*
Gentles, come, come one and all,
And claim a lady, etc.

BEARNE:
Fortune's the mistress of our feast,
And howso blind or mad her rule,
Still gives she most unto the least,
For Fortune ever favors the fool.
So I, the poorest of all those here,
Am rich only in hope, and see
That Fortune will surely be my dear,
If I choose the color of hope. For me—
There's no choice but green.

CINTIA:
                    (If I have to pick
Some other color than Carlos might name,
I'm sure I'd much rather stick
With Bearne.) I have the same
Color, I'm green, and I'm yours for the dance.
(She gives him the green sash.)

1405

1410

1415

1420

1425

1430

BEARNE:

Your favor, lady, crowns my joys.   1435
Fortune gave you to me; yet if chance
Had not, I'd have taken you by choice.
*(They dance a turn, then putting on half-masks, withdraw to one side
staying on their feet.)*
MUSICIANS: *(Singing)*
Long live the men of hope—godspeed!
Their lives are sure the best,
For hope is all they think they need,   1440
To count themselves as blest.
Fa-la-ra-la, fa-la-ra-la, etc.
GASTÓN:

Hope may run some men's lives—but mine
Has always been ruled by jealousy:
By the fear your star should brighter shine   1445
On others than it does on me.
Jealousy's my passion, and
I choose her color—blue.
FENISA:
                                And you
Get me, I'm blue. Take it from my hand.
(She gives him the blue sash.)
GASTÓN:

Chameleon-like I change my hue.   1450
For, Lady, such luck you bring my way,
That all my jealousy fades away.
(They dance and draw aside.)
MUSICIANS: *(Singing)*
The jealous man is never free
Even when he wins the prize;
For then he must fight the jealousy   1455
That burns in others' eyes.
Fa-la-ra-la, fa-la-ra-la, etc.
POLILLA:

And I—do I pick a color too?
DIANA:

You do.

POLILLA:

                  I need one—my color just went
Right out of my face and flew   1460
Away in sheer embarrassment.

DIANA:

What color do you want?

POLILLA:

                       I've got
A taste for ladies whose looks are plain;
The girl I usually get is not
What I'd call pretty. Now in your train,   1465
I see only the fairest kind
Of ladies, every one a rose.
Where in all this bouquet can I find
The absolute worst, which everyone knows,
Is my due by fate? If she's got to be   1470
A rose, I can only suppose
She'll be a dried one. So come to me,
Where are you, my desert rose?

LAURA:

I'm here, I'm rose. I'm yours, you see.
(She gives him the sash.)

POLILLA:

So I'm obliged to be nice today,   1475
And you're obliged to make love to me?

LAURA:

The other way round.

POLILLA:

                Turnabout's fair play.
But will you love me back, if I do?

LAURA:

Nothing will happen, you little beast,
Unless you start—it's up to you.   1480

POLILLA:

Me? All right. In a well-greased
Frying pan, butter may melt
And whiten, yet its pale hue
Is shamed by yours. Your lovely pelt

Is softer than a dishrag, and you 1485
Have eyes whose whiteness, once displayed,
Shines brighter than two bars of soap.
Seven of the loveliest mouths laid
End to end can never hope
To equal one of yours. I'll leave 1490
Your legs and feet alone; they wear
Much finer threads than my wits can weave.
And to conclude, your beauty's a snare,
And like Adam and Eve I've fallen in,
Though falling for you doesn't count as a sin. 1495
(They dance a turn and withdraw.)
MUSICIANS: *(Singing)*
The man who turns from blooming flowers
To pluck the rose that's dried,
Will find true love in his rosy bowers,
And the prick of the thorn beside.
Fa-la-ra-la, fa-la-ra-la, etc. 1500
CARLOS:
To make my choice, I am the last,
Noblesse oblige obliges me,
The force of duty binds me fast
To play my part in this comedy.
And since 'tis agony and pain 1505
To go against the heart's desire,
Of all the colors that remain,
I choose the one that stands for ire:
Mother-of-pearl's my choice, Is there
A lady for me?
DIANA:
                    I am for you. 1510
Mother-of-pearl's the color I wear.
(She gives him a sash of that color.)
CARLOS:
Lady, if I only knew
What my hap would be today,
I'd never have forced myself to plead
For your love in sport. For now I may 1515

Be forced to fall in love indeed.
(They dance a turn and withdraw.)
MUSICIANS: *(Singing)*
Mother-of-pearl may be the sign
Of burning wrath and ire.
But there's no heat in cold disdain,
While love, like hate, is born of fire.   1520
Fa-la-ra-la, fa-la-ra-la, etc.
POLILLA: *(Aside)*
So now at last you can stuff your cheeks
With delicacies till they bulge.
You can eat in a day what would feed you for weeks,
Just be careful—don't overindulge.   1525
DIANA:
Let the musicians lead the way
To the room where we hold the ball;
And there let the ladies and gentlemen pay
Each other the debt of Carnival.
MUSICIANS: *(Singing)*
Gentles come, come one and all,   1530
With your ladies by your sides,
This is the feast of Carnival,
When Love is in disguise.
Fa-la-ra-la, fa-la-ra-la, etc.
*(They go out two by two, and at the doorway, Diana and Carlos
stay behind.)*
DIANA:
(I've got to get even with this man,   1535
Or all the world will mock at me.)
You're a very different wooer, sir,
And from your diffidence, I see
That you make love upon compulsion;
And when you're forced to play at it,   1540
You fail because you don't know how.
It's not a failure of love, but of wit.
CARLOS:
If I were only playing at love,
I wouldn't be so diffident;

A wagging tongue is always the sign   1545
Of a lack of sentiment.
DIANA:
Then speak, are you in love with me?
CARLOS:
If I were not in love with you,
Why would I tremble so with fear?
DIANA:
What are you saying? Are you speaking true?   1550
CARLOS:
What the soul wishes the world to know,
How can the tongue ever belie?
DIANA:
But aren't you the man who said to me
That you could never love?
CARLOS:
                          That was I!
But I had not been infected yet   1555
By the poison from a certain dart.
DIANA:
What dart is that?
CARLOS:
                     That hand of yours,
That pierced me to the very heart.
And like the fish that sends a drop
Of mortal venom up the line   1560
And along the rod onto the hand,
Which stuns the arm that reels him in,
And paralyzes the fisherman,
So to my very soul there crept
The sweet inflaming poison which   1565
From off your beauteous hand has leapt
Onto mine, coursing from thence through all
My veins, and reaching at last my heart.
DIANA:
(Rejoice, my wit, I've paid him back,
His pride has fallen to my art!   1570
Now beauty wields the whip of disdain,

Whose biting lash this fool must feel!)
What's this? You who could never imagine
Yourself in love, do you love for real?

CARLOS:
My soul is bursting into flames,   1575
Thunderbolts beat against my breast;
Have mercy on me and cool this rag-
ing fire that will not give me rest.

DIANA:
Let go! What do you mean? Let go!
(She drops her mask and pulls back her hand.)
Have mercy on you? There's mitigation   1580
In the blindness of your passion—I'll spare you
The rod, but not the humiliation.
So now you ask me for my favor.
Claiming to love me truthfully.

CARLOS:
(Good Lord, I nearly lost my head;   1585
Thank God I've got a remedy!)

DIANA:
Don't you remember when I said
That the price you'd pay for loving me
Would be to suffer all my scorn,
And get not an ounce of sympathy?   1590

CARLOS:
Oh, are you telling the truth right now?

DIANA:
Aren't you truly in love with me?

CARLOS:
Who me, Milady? Could a leopard
Change his spots so easily?
Am I truly in love? What, lady, I?   1595
Good lord, what a thought! How could your beauty
Ever conceive such a thing? In love?
Me? Lady, this is just a duty.
If I ever do fall in love,
I'll be too ashamed to speak. What I said   1600
Just now was to meet my obligation.

DIANA:

What are you saying? I wish I were dead!
You mean it's not true? What did you say?
How can I make—? (I can't even speak—
My pride is—This is humiliating—)　　　　　　　　　1605

CARLOS:

I would never have thought your discretion so weak
That it could be fooled by my pretending.

DIANA:

But all this business about the dart,
And the fish and the line and rod and all that,
And saying the coldness of your heart　　　　　　　1610
Was only because you hadn't been touched
By the powerful poison of love?

CARLOS:

Yes, that was rather good, I thought.
You wanted me to talk to you of
Affection—I'm not such a fool to think　　　　　　1615
I could do it without a little detail!

DIANA:

(Good lord, what's happening to me?
Am I such a fool that he can rail
At me like this, and I deserve it?
His burning insult is the flame　　　　　　　　　　1620
That sets my very soul on fire;
And now, I fear, he knows my shame.
I've got to make him fall in love,
Though it cost me my immortal soul.)

CARLOS:

Milady, they're waiting for us in there.　　　　　　1625

DIANA:

(How can I be such a stupid fool!)
I'm sorry, sir, did you—

CARLOS:

　　　　　　　　　　　Excuse me?

DIANA:

(What shall I do? I'm going blind.)

Shall we put on our masks and go inside?

CARLOS:
(That didn't turn out too badly, I find.
But is that how she treats a confession of love?   1630
That cruel, inhuman, savage breast!
I'll heap upon my raging flames
The snows that crown Mt. Etna's crest!)

DIANA:
I see you're a man of enormous wit,   1635
To play at love so persuasively
That I took your feigning for the truth.

CARLOS:
Oh that was just a courtesy
Of yours, to feign that you were fooled—
'Twas a friendly way of favoring me;   1640
Fulfilling the debt of Carnival,
Maintaining your integrity,
And meeting with an easy grace
The festive obligation.
And by pretending to be caught   1645
You gave my wit your approbation,
Preferring ingenuity
To easy affectation.

DIANA:
(That was a very clever way
Of telling me I was a fool;   1650
But I can fool him back—just so!)
I knew it all the time, but you'll
Still have to keep pretending, sir;
Go on, then, since it may constrain
My heart to like you more.

CARLOS:
                        But how?   1655

DIANA:
Because to conquer my disdain,
Wit has far more force than love,
And obliges me to make reply.

CARLOS:
(You're not too hard to figure out;
Suppose I let the arrow fly
Back at you?)
DIANA:
            Pray, continue. 1660
CARLOS:
                         No,
Milady.
DIANA:
    Why?
CARLOS:
              It hurts so much
To hear you say that you're obliged
To me. I'm afraid I've lost my touch
For keeping up this mask of love. 1665
DIANA:
Whatever could you lose by it,
If the only thing that obliges me
Is but the service of your wit?
CARLOS:
There is the danger of being loved.
DIANA:
Is it so bad to be loved by me? 1670
CARLOS:
It would be out of my control;
And if I found myself to be
The object of love, I'd rather die.
DIANA:
(What my beauty must listen to!)
How could you even dare to presume 1675
That I could fall in love with you?
CARLOS:
You said yourself that being nice
Was close to love. It seems to me,
If you admit you like me, well—
How far from love can liking be? 1680

DIANA:

Not nearly as close as you've already come
In your foolish pride to insulting me.
So near in fact, and yet so far
Already past common courtesy,
That I would only forgive you if   1685
You leave me at once.

CARLOS:

                    But how shall we
Excuse our absence from the feast?
Think of the scandal that would be!

DIANA:

I'm willing to take the risk of that.
Say that a sudden infirmity   1690
Has left me feeling indisposed.

CARLOS:

You give me leave to leave you be?
I'm free to leave the party then?

DIANA:

Go when I bid you, 'tis my command!

CARLOS:

And the greatest favor your grace can give;   1695
I leave you, ma'am, in the good Lord's hand.
(He goes out.)

DIANA:

What on earth's going on with me?
I feel so blind and mortified,
That if I knew there was a way
To triumph over that man's pride,   1700
Even at the risk of my good name,
To insure my beauty's victory,
I'd pay any price, even the cost
Of my own respectability.
(Enter Polilla.)

POLILLA:

What's wrong, milady, has something occurred   1705
To spoil our sweet festivity?

DIANA:

I've given myself a tiny hurt.

POLILLA:

If it's on the head, make a plaster
From the bark of a tacamaca tree,
And rub your legs faster and faster.   1710

DIANA:

Ladies don't have legs, they have limbs.

POLILLA:

That's why you use bark from a tree,
For aching limbs, it's just the thing.
But where did you hurt yourself, let me see.

DIANA:

Somewhere around the heart.   1715

POLILLA:

Lord, if that's all that's wrong with you,
We'll bleed you a little, when give you a purge,
And then apply a leech or two,
To suck out a couple of dozen cups
Of nice red blood, you'll be tight as a drum.   1720

DIANA:

Satin, it's so humiliating
Not to be able to overcome
His diffidence.

POLILLA:

            Do you doubt yourself?
So you'd ruin him, with no regrets?

DIANA:

None! But how can the man be ruined?   1725

POLILLA:

Publish a list of all his debts.
But seriously, don't you mean
That what you're really thinking of,
Is making him fall in love with you?

DIANA:

To see that man dying of love,   1730
I'd give up every jewel in my crown.

POLILLA:

Is that your spite or your tenderness talking? Carlitos getting under your skin?

DIANA:

What tenderness? I'm solid rock!
I'll burn him to ash with my contempt,   1735
And scorn and fury and hate and spleen—
That's all I want.

POLILLA:

            (She's in for it now!
This fig is still a little green,
But sure as there are boys and stones,
She'll ripen into something sweet.)   1740

DIANA:

I know how fond the fool can be
Of singing.

POLILLA:

           Yes, the lively beat
Of Gregorian chant, or a lovely psalm
Accompanied by castanets.

DIANA:

A psalm—what are you talking about?   1745

POLILLA:

It's the very thing that always gets
Him going. One rousing verse of a Latin
Motet puts him in such a state!

DIANA:

I need you to do me a favor, Satin.

POLILLA:

What's that?

DIANA:

           You know the little gate,   1750
That leads to my garden? Open it.
My ladies and I will all be there,
And we'll be singing—nothing to do
With him—and then you put him where
He can hear us sing, and tell him that   1755
He needn't worry if he gets caught,
Since you're the only one we'll blame.

POLILLA:

Oh, this is quite the little plot—

Because the minute he hears you sing
He'll turn to jelly at the sound. 1760
DIANA:
Go fetch him here right now.
POLILLA:
Like a dog on a leash I'll bring him around.
The man's been known to go to funerals
Just to hear the choir. Speaking of them,
Pick something sweet.
DIANA:
                                   What do you mean? 1765
POLILLA:
The song you sing—make it a gem;
Catchy lyrics, bouncy tune.
DIANA:
Like what?
POLILLA:
                        A plainchant *requiem*.
DIANA:
I'm going into the garden now.
POLILLA:
Said Eve to Adam, in all her glory, 1770
To bring him to a second Fall.
DIANA:
I'll wait for you there.
(She leaves.)
POLILLA:
                        It's the same old story!
You get to be the forbidden fruit,
And I'm the snake who helps you do't.
Gentlemen, it's a sorry sight 1775
When a princess loses her wits and all;
I guess it's like the proverb says,
The bigger they come the harder they fall.
It's like trying to eat a single cherry,
When a lady starts to lose her wits; 1780
You say to yourself, I'll just take one,
And you end up with a pile of pits!

66 Spite for Spite

(Carlos comes in.)

CARLOS:
Moth, my friend!

POLILLA:
       I've got some good news, master.

CARLOS:
Has something happened?

POLILLA:
      You might say so—we've smashed her!

CARLOS:
How do you know? What did she say to you?   1785

POLILLA:
To entice you to love her, she gave me a job to do:
To bring you to the garden, where you're to spy
Her shining brighter than any star in the sky,
And singing with her ladies.
Which she supposes is her only course   1790
To soften such a hardened heart as yours.

CARLOS:
That's it? Good Lord, you astonish me!

POLILLA:
The lady's tremendously light, you see,
And stoneblind as well! There's no room for doubt.
Look what she's doing and who she's got helping her out. 1795
(Music within.)

CARLOS:
I hear the music playing.

POLILLA:
      She's crazy for you!

CARLOS:
Hush up, they're singing now.

POLILLA:
      Well, hallelu!

LADIES: *(Within, singing)*
 The waves they were of sapphire,
On the bosom of the sea,
And as they rolled, the waters sang   1800
That he was their king to be.

POLILLA:
Let's go inside.
CARLOS:
What do you mean? I'll die!
POLILLA:
Leave dying for the shepherds in romance.
Let's go inside. You've got to give it a try.
CARLOS:
But what should I do?
POLILLA:
Go in, don't even glance   1805
Her way, amuse yourself with the lushest part
Of the garden, let the lady sing her heart
To shreds, don't even listen, don't give her a chance,
She'll fry herself to a crisp.
CARLOS:
I just can't do it.
POLILLA:
Good Lord, why not? I've got to put you through it,   1810
Or, sir, I'll take the dagger that I wear
And put it through you. You've got it bad, I swear,
And the cure is bound to cause some pain.
CARLOS:
Don't promise
Where you never mean to pay, my lad.
POLILLA:
I'm sorry that the medicine tastes so bad,   1815
But, sir, your soul's infected through and through.
CARLOS:
They're singing again, listen, I beg of you.
POLILLA:
Let's go, or my soul be damned for it,
We're wasting time.
CARLOS:
Oh, we'll just wait a bit
And then we'll go inside.

POLILLA:
                              You'll be able to hear her   1820
Much better inside. You should go nearer.
(Or go to hell!)
CARLOS:
                    But first we ought
To listen.
POLILLA:
          Go in!
CARLOS:
                  Listen!
POLILLA:
                    I'd rather not!
(He gives him a push offstage.)
(Diana and all her ladies enter in petticoats and camisoles.)
LADIES: (Singing)
The waves they were of sapphire
On the bosom of the sea,   1825
And as they rolled, the waters sang
That he was their king to be.
DIANA:
Did anyone see Carlos come in?
CINTIA:
Not only haven't we seen him here,
We haven't even seen a sign   1830
Of him in the garden anywhere.
DIANA:
Laura, find out if he's nearby.
LAURA:
I think I see him by the fence.
DIANA:
I'd risk the ruin of my reputation
To conquer that man's diffidence.   1835
LAURA:
Surely, milady, your beauty is such,
That a man would have to be a nin-
ny not to love you at first sight,
I see him, lady, he's coming in,

He's coming in!

DIANA:
What did you say? 1840

LAURA:
He and Satin are wandering
This way.

DIANA:
Come on and sit with me,
And everyone begin to sing.
(They sit, and Carlos and Polilla enter.)

POLILLA:
Don't weaken, sir, don't soften now!

CARLOS:
Oh Moth, look at her loveliness, 1845
It's miraculous! She bewitches me
Even in the simplest dress.

POLILLA:
Women always look their best
In camisoles and underskirts.

CARLOS:
She needs no frills, when without them, she's 1850
So beautiful it almost hurts.

POLILLA:
You're right, they're just like artichokes,
In a smart greengrocer's store.
He leaves the prickly leaves stuck on
Because they make the thing weigh more, 1855
And raise the price to the customer,
Although they play no other part.
You buy it, get it home, and then
Strip off the leaves and eat the heart.
That's what it's like with women, sir, 1860
You eat the part you're seeing now,
And all those ribbons and overskirts
Are scraps you feed the family cow.
Just turn your face the other way—
You're lost if you look back at her! 1865

CARLOS:
Oh Moth, I just can't help myself.

POLILLA:
What do you mean you can't? I swear,
You'll end up with a knife in your face
If you turn now.
(He holds the dagger up to his face.)

CARLOS:
I'm not turning round.

POLILLA:
But I can see you listening, sir,   1870
Traps can be laid both for sight and sound.

CARLOS:
Then let's go a little farther off,
So when she sings, I can beg her pardon
For ignoring her, because I was
Entranced by the beauty of her garden.   1875

CINTIA:
He's listening, begin to sing!

DIANA:
Now see if his heart will harden!

LADIES: *(Singing)*
When lovely May goes gathering
The sweetest April flowers,
She weaves herself a crown of hope,   1880
To pass the lonely hours.

DIANA:
Has he come back to listen?

LAURA:
                              No.

DIANA:
Why not? Perhaps he couldn't hear.

LAURA:
It's possible, he's far away.

CARLOS:
The way this garden's laid out is sheer   1885
Genius. I've never seen the like.

POLILLA:
Look at this—it's absolutely dear!

DIANA:
He's looking at my garden—what
Is this? Has he got any sense?
Sing louder, ladies, let us see
If that makes any difference.

LADIES: *(Singing)*
The sweetest flowers of the month,
Upon her head be put;
And only the brightest blossoms
Should kiss her conquering foot.

CARLOS:
Look how this flower-bed is shaped
Like her coat of arms. How cleverly!

POLILLA:
And this is even smarter still.

DIANA:
What do I hear? What do I see?
My flowerbeds are being praised
While I am signing!

CARLOS:
                I've never seen
Ivy so wittily intertwined.
What an amazing shade of green!

POLILLA:
Greens that look good enough to eat!

DIANA:
It's just that he is out of range.
Laura, tell him he's failed to notice
That I am here.
(Laura rises.)

CINTIA:
            (This is quite a change—
She's rushing headlong into love!)

LAURA:
Carlos, I'm to let you know
My mistress Diana's over there.

CARLOS:
This place is famous high and low

1890

1895

1900

1905

1910

For the beauty of its laurel grove.
But frankly I find that cherrytree
Destroys that stand of hyacinths.

POLILLA:
A cherrytree is a sight to see!   1915

DIANA:
So, Laura, did you let him know?

LAURA:
I told him everything, I vow.

DIANA:
So it's not for want of knowing then—
Tell me what he's doing now.
(The men pass in front of the women, Polilla holding his dagger to Carlos's face to keep him from turning around.)

POLILLA:
All right, now try to walk this way   1920
Without looking around.

CARLOS:
           Don't take
Me there! I'm far too weak. I'm too
Afraid to go!

POLILLA:
           For heaven's sake,
Don't move your head—my dagger's there!

CARLOS:
I just can't help myself, my friend.   1925

POLILLA:
Look out, you're about to impale yourself.

CARLOS:
What do you want? I can't defend
Myself.

POLILLA:
        And now we'll go another way.

CARLOS:
This way, you mean?

POLILLA:
           No, that way—there!

DIANA:
Did he come back?

LAURA:

He's not planning to. 1930

DIANA:
I can't believe what I'm seeing here.
Fenisa, wander over his way
And give him a little message from me.
(Fenisa gets up.)

POLILLA:
She's firing off another round;
It'll be another dud, you'll see. 1935

FENISA:
Carlos?

CARLOS:

Yes?

POLILLA:

Did someone call?

FENISA:
You see that Diana's looking this way?

CARLOS:
I was so entranced by this fountain here,
And a lovely fountain it is, I'd say—
That I never saw Her Highness there; 1940
Tell her I'll leave as fast as I can.

DIANA:
Good Lord, I think he's actually leaving!
Listen, I'm talking to you, young man!

CARLOS:
To me, milady?

DIANA:

Yes, to you!

CARLOS:
What's your command?

DIANA:

How could you dare 1945
To bring yourself inside these walls,
When clearly you knew that this was where

My ladies and I had come to retire?

CARLOS:
I was so impressed by your lovely garden,
That I never even saw you here,   1950
And all I can do is beg your pardon.

DIANA:
(Worse and worse—he won't even say
He came in here to hear me sing!)
But didn't you hear me?

CARLOS:
                          Lady, no.

DIANA:
Impossible.

CARLOS:
          It's a foolish thing   1955
I've done. So let me make amends
By removing myself and my offense.
(He goes out.)

CINTIA:
Lady, the man is as dumb as a post!

DIANA:
Go away! His indifference
Is enough to drive me out of my mind!   1960

CINTIA: (Aside to Laura)
Laura, I'd say the game is done.

LAURA: (Aside to Cintia)
If she's not in love with Carlos now,
She will be very soon.
(They go out.)

DIANA:
Heavens! What is this I'm feeling!
I'm like a volcano ready to blow.   1965
The man insulted me!

POLILLA: (Aside)
                     It's true—
Poor soul, I can smell the lava flow!

DIANA:
Satin!

POLILLA:
> Yes, ma'am, what can I do?

DIANA:
What's going on? I thought that he
Had come to hear me sing.

POLILLA:
> He did.   1970

DIANA:
But he didn't come back to listen to me!

POLILLA:
Lady, the man should be committed.

DIANA:
What did he say, did he give an excuse?

POLILLA:
I'm too embarrassed.

DIANA:
> Tell me, then.

POLILLA:
He said you sang with all the mus-   1975
icality of a schoolboy choir.
He couldn't bear it.

DIANA:
> That's what he said?

POLILLA:
Yes, ma'am.

DIANA:
> Did he mean it as an insult?

POLILLA:
He's a boob.

DIANA:
> I'm going out of my head!

POLILLA:
Now there's no reason to—

DIANA:
> I'm dying!   1980

POLILLA:
He's a philistine.

DIANA:

>For that, I commit

Myself to seek revenge, although
I have to die pursuing it.
(She goes out.)
POLILLA:
Roll up the rugs, it's gonna start hoppin' in here
Higher than hailstones off a horses rear!

Act Three

(Enter Carlos, Polilla, Don Gastón, and the Count of Bearne.)

BEARNE:
 Carlos, because of our friendship, we feel we may
Make use of you, in this plan we've designed.

CARLOS:
You know already, my friends, I'm bound to obey.

BEARNE:
 I'm sure you are, so I open to you my mind.

POLILLA:
So open already and let the thought go,   1990
All of this build-up's a terrible grind.

BEARNE:
 There isn't a feast, or a finery, or a show
Of courtship, or an exhibition of delight
That the three of us haven't already tried, you know,
 In order to conquer this woman's confounded spite   1995
Towards all of us, that's made Diana treat us
Even as kindly as common courtesy might.
 You've had your go at her, luck let you beat us,
Yet she tramples on custom, on the dictates of chance,
And by ignoring you, she will defeat us   2000
 All. She has turned the pleasure of the dance
To sorrow, and all the ladies' laughs to sighs,
And us to fools, if you consider the circumstance.
 And now our reputations we must prize
Above our loves; it's a moral obligation that we   2005
Must conquer the folly of those disdainful eyes;
 And the pleasure of paying that debt will be
A joy for us all, if we could see her brought
To grief by the efforts of any one of us three.
 Accordingly, we've hatched a little plot,   2010
Have Don Gastón and I, which we will share
With you, and if this arrow wounds her not,
 We see no other way of getting there.

CARLOS:
So what's the plot?

GASTÓN:
                    Each of us for the next few days,
Is already matched by chance with his lady fair,   2015
 So we'll pursue them with our courtly ways,
And give Diana not so much as a thought;
She and her disdain have withdrawn from our gaze,
 And if her highness returns to see how haut-
iness has cost her so much adoration,   2020
She'll feel the sting of wounded pride, if not
 Of love. If we see any indication
That she feels hurt, our wooing must be bold-
er, til her pride turns to humiliation.

POLILLA:
 Not a bad prescription, sirs, however old: 2025
I've often heard of doctors using it;
They feed a fever, but they always starve a cold.

BEARNE:
 And if this remedy should fail, if a bit
Of her own medicine won't cure the malady
Or soothe it, at least it won't increase the fit.   2030
 If Diana takes offense at the decency
With which we woo her, she'll only be more upset
If we persist, and increase her obstinacy.
 There's no way left for us—except to let
Her alone, and then the law of Nature will take   2035
Its course, and we'll have Diana in our debt.
 For when she finds that men no longer make
A fuss over her, the same ones she loved to spurn,
She's bound to take offense—for her beauty's sake.
 She'll miss all the attention, and she'll yearn   2040
For the very thing she was too cool
To care about before. Her soul will burn
 To have it, her pride demand it. Her cruel
Heart will never confess it, no, but she'll
Be forced to admit to herself that she's a fool.   2045
 And still her mind will refuse to give in. And we'll
Have our revenge; for when her intellect
Won't yield to love—what torment she will feel!

CARLOS:

What you propose, from wounded self-respect,
I too will undertake, for reasons of   2050
My own: first, and foremost, she must expect
No less; she's forcing us to rise above
Her cold disdain. And secondly, how can
Her spite hurt me, who never mean to love?

BEARNE:

I take your word.

CARLOS:

                I give it as a man.   2055

BEARNE:

Of our own free will, we forbid our lips to speak
Her name. From this time forth, no more Dian—

GASTÓN:

Against her spite all other means are weak.

CARLOS:

And her I bind myself to do the right.

BEARNE:

And you shall see what vengeance we shall wreak.   2060

GASTÓN:

And though Diana may find it impolite,
Let's go increase the attentions that we pay
To our ladies fair.

CARLOS:

            It's crazy, but it might
Just work.

BEARNE:

             If we all ignore her at once, I'd say
We'll vanquish her for sure.

CARLOS:

              I agree with you.   2065

BEARNE:

Let's go then, Don Gastón!

GASTÓN:

              Bearne, away!

BEARNE:

Your help will make our wishes all come true.

(Bearne and Gastón go out.)

POLILLA:
This is the best plan I've ever heard,
Their help will make *your* wish come true;
They've offered to beat the bushes for you, 2070
So you can take a shot at the bird.

CARLOS:
She's terrifying! Even when she's beat-
en, she won't give in to her heart's desire!

POLILLA:
I tell you sir, the woman's on fire;
But she doesn't know how to admit defeat! 2075
There's one thing you can be certain of,
She loves you though she says she doesn't;
What looked like hate, sir, really wasn't;
It was the quintessence of love.
When you give a woman a terrible dose 2080
Of disdain, and Diana got it bad,
I suppose you could say that it makes her mad,
But mad for love's what I'd diagnose.
She talks of vengeance night and day
For the pain you're putting her through, 2085
But don't think for a moment she's through with you;
She'll come around very nicely I'd say.

CARLOS:
What does she say?

POLILLA:
                              That you're to blame,
That you're a fool and an idiot,
A blockhead, an inconsiderate 2090
Boor, but I know how to play that game,
And I say, "Yes, ma'am, the man is mad,
And completely rotten," and she'll turn round
And take your part and say, "You scound-
rel, no, he's not, he's not so bad!" 2095
And now, since waiting seems to be
A complete dead end, I think she'll try
Another way to get at you, by

Goading your heart to jealousy.
 So now you know the sharp little prick   2100
She's aiming to stick in you.
And if it stings, what you have to do
Is laugh and lie and say, "That tick-
 les"; and she'll come running when you call.
CARLOS:
But why?
POLILLA:
             It may kill her, but I know   2105
If she plants that seed, and it doesn't grow,
She'll be on her knees like a beggar bawl-
 ing for a handout. Sir, I can cite
Authority—Lope de Vega, for one—
The Spanish Phoenix, that bright sun   2110
In our literary skies—didn't he write:
 "The jealous man that doth offend,
What's his true end?
But taking vengeance for a slight,
Which if it goeth not right,   2115
To buy back love, he will all spend"?
 But listen, the princes are coming in,
With the music they've arranged to play.
CARLOS:
I think I'll join them on their way.
POLILLA:
And let the games begin.   2120
CARLOS:
Diana's coming.
POLILLA:
             Be careful, sir,
Get out of sight.
CARLOS:
             I'll go over there.
(Carlos goes off.)
POLILLA:
Then go—if the pack of them spots us here,
We'll lose this trick, and be back where we were.

(Music within, and Diana comes walking out.)
MUSICIANS: *(Singing, off)*
O Shepherds, Cintia me hath slain,   2125
In Cintia I live and die;
I live to see her lovely face,
And find my death in her cold eye.
DIANA:
 All this for Cintia?
POLILLA:
                    It's the mating-call
Of the Bearnes.
DIANA:
                    Well, isn't that nice?   2130
POLILLA: *(Aside)*
And this just adds a little spice
To the stew of love, that's all.
DIANA:
 I'd rather not witness this rivalry
Where men flatter women with fancy names.
I wish they'd take their Carnival games   2135
Somewhere else and leave me be.
POLILLA:
 Beware, milady, of the danger
Of being too harsh a tyrant. Though you
Won't love, forbidding others to
Is simply playing the dog in the manger.   2140
DIANA:
 But having to hear one precious song
After another of Cintia, Laur-
a, Fenisa, don't you find it bor-
ing in the extreme?
POLILLA:
                    If you think it's wrong,
 If it upsets you to find your name   2145
In a song, and you won't be Dianafied,
Let them be Cintisized or *Feni*sied,
Or Laureated—what's to blame?
 Bearne's so taken with little Miss

Cintia, that he says his heart is hers, 2150
And he's written some rather impressive verse.
DIANA:
And what does he say?
POLILLA:

          It goes something like this:
  "Shall I accuse my Cintia of a sin?
Thou shalt not kill, the commandments say,
Yet Cintia slays me every day; 2155
Sinless with her have I ever been,
For sin and Cintia can be no kin.
Yet since my Cintia has power to raise
From the cinders of dying love a blaze
By the scintillation of her eye, 2160
And rescind her doom, I woo her by
This *sin*cere poem of my praise."
DIANA:
 Very pretty I'm sure. But there's the strain
Of some other music.
POLILLA:

          A serenade.
DIANA:
Something some other lover has made. 2165
POLILLA: *(Aside)*
She's practically exploding with pain.
MUSICIANS: *(Singing, off)*
 Though my Fenisa takes her name
From the bird that rises from the dead,
She's far more potent than the Phoenix,
For she gives out life and death instead. 2170
DIANA:
 Well, aren't they just the sweetest!
POLILLA:

         Oh, Geez!
Pretty impressive, but mine's got more spirit.
I wrote something for Laura, wanna hear it?
DIANA:
So *you're* writing music now?

POLILLA:
                    Silence pu-leaze!
Who is Laura, what is she?   2175
Another name for a laurel tree.
And I'm a fish swimming in her bay,
Marinating the live-long day.

DIANA:
  But what of Carlos, where's my song?
Or isn't it something he's capable of?   2180

POLILLA:
If he'd ever manage to fall in love
He'd be here now, doing you wrong.
  But he says he can't, and you seemed to be
Singing the same tune, to send him away;
Your *vaya con dios* the other day   2185
He took as a kind of divine decree.

DIANA:
  I grant that what you say is true,
But surely he could have persisted with me,
Persistence would have been courtesy.

POLILLA:
Was that a thing he would ever do?   2190
  They'll all be coming to the big affair.
He'll need a partner for the celebration—
Since going alone's a humiliation—
And you've refused to join him there.

DIANA:
  I could go with him to the ball: 2195
But you're not suggesting that I should?

POLILLA:
Ah, what does he know of should or could?
He's not too good at protocol.
  Already the ladies and gentlemen
Are arriving for the ball.   2200
The garlands and the plumes they wear
Make springtime in your hall.

DIANA:
  They're coming inside with their ladies,

And Carlos is with them all.
POLILLA: *(Aside)*
My friends, as sure as God's above,   2205
Their coldness to her will either provoke her
To swallow her pride and fall in love—
Or it'll get stuck in her throat and choke 'er.
(All the Gentlemen enter with their Ladies, all in hats covered with plumes.)
MUSICIANS: *(Singing)*
 When Cupid wants to honor those
He hurts, he always chooses   2210
To put the brightest feathers
In the arrows that he uses.
BEARNE:
Princes, this is our very last chance,
To sting this woman with love's sweet pain.
GASTÓN:
But always like perfect gentlemen.   2215
CARLOS:
My courtesy will be perfect—disdain.
BEARNE:
My lovely Cintia, every second,
I seem to forget that I am yours;
I can scarce believe that fickle Fortune
Laid this blessing at my doors.   2220
CINTIA:
I too have doubts, and can only think
Such fine words issue from the debt
You owe to the day, and not from love.
BEARNE:
Then I heartily pray the sun may set,
The day may end, and with it your doubts.   2225
GASTÓN:
And you, Fenisa, if you doubt as well,
You will see my gallantry ascend
To heights unknown in heaven or hell,
When all that remains is the single tribute
Of faith with which I worship you.   2230

DIANA:
No one's paying attention to me!

POLILLA:
And I don't care what happens to
Any of them, except for that
Milksop, Carlos the Magnificent.
And what is he? not much, except   2235
The kindest and most valiant,
Most courteous and most discreet—
Why the poems that he could write would be
Masterpieces—a prince among men!
But we can't do much with that, can we?   2240

BEARNE:
My dear Count Fox, we mustn't waste
A moment. I can't wait to present
The festivities we've planned!

GASTÓN:
Let's make this the happiest day we've spent!

DIANA:
How tender they've become.

POLILLA:
                        Milksops!   2245

DIANA:
But tenderness isn't so bad a thing!

POLILLA:
Not if you're a capon, maybe.

BEARNE:
On with the music, come now, sing!
And celebrate our happiness!

CARLOS:
I'm drawn like a magnet to their echoing!   2250
(They all pass by Diana, without paying her any attention.)

MUSICIANS: *(Singing)*
 When Cupid wants to honor those
He hurts, he always chooses, etc.

DIANA:
How solemn they are, and how polite!

POLILLA:
You know what they look like to me?
DIANA:
No, what?
POLILLA:

A bunch of monks and nuns.   2255
DIANA:
And Carlos is going with them, you see?
All I feel for him is disdain;
But this is a perfect moment to
Inflame his heart with jealousy.
You call him.
POLILLA:

Sir! Yoo-hoo!   2260
CARLOS:
Who calls?
POLILLA:

Appropinquacción
Ad parlandum.
CARLOS:

With whom, pray?
POLILLA:

Mécum.
CARLOS:
But how could you call me now, my friend?
Lovers must go where love would take 'em,
And you see I'm in love with this song.   2265
DIANA:
You are in love? Well, isn't that charm-
ing? In love with whom?
CARLOS:

Why, ma'am,
With the very lady here on my arm.
DIANA:
What lady?
CARLOS:

Lady Liberty.
Whose partner I am today.   2270

DIANA:
Oh! Of course! (For a moment there
He frightened me.)
POLILLA: *(Aside)*
      That's the way!
From here it's just a hop and a skip,
Like a trip to Toledo from Madrid.
DIANA:
Your partner is Lady Liberty? 2275
You have very exalted taste, indeed.
CARLOS:
In matter of taste, it matters not
How high or low one may aspire.
For taste is voluntary, and the will
Need give no reason for her desire. 2280
DIANA:
But here there is no will involved.
CARLOS:
But there is.
DIANA:
      Well, either I'm misus-
ing the word or this isn't will. Free will
Requires there must be something to choose.
CARLOS:
There is! Not loving is my choice. 2285
My will commits itself to this.
By choosing not to love, I will
The act of lovelessness.
DIANA:
But negatives have no existence;
They're only fictions of the mind, 2290
Abstractions whose very being
Is hypothetically defined.
And even so is this will of yours—
Without a cause there's no effect.
CARLOS:
And you, my lady, have no idea 2295
Of what it is to love. I suspect

The nicest thing that I could say
Is that you're way in over your head.
DIANA:
Not really, sir, the reason need
Not suffer effects; it can be led 2300
To find out causes by other means.
Philosophy can make its way
Without experience—and yet
I think I've found the knowledge today
That comes from experience as well. 2305
CARLOS:
Are you in love?
DIANA:
                    I long to be.
POLILLA: (Aside to Carlos)
Careful, you're getting awfully close
To the nets of jealousy.
You better rub yourself all over
With the finest oil of disdain 2310
If you want to slip out of that noose.
DIANA: (Aside)
If he's got even half a brain,
He'll go up in flames—or he's no man.
POLILLA: (Aside)
And it would happen exactly that way,
If I hadn't warned him to be on his guard. 2315
CARLOS:
I'm dying to hear what you have to say.
DIANA:
Carlos, I've come to recognize
That the opinion I've professed
Is contrary to reason, to
My country's interest, 2320
The security of my people and
The continuance of my crown.
In view of all these dangers,
I have beaten my reason down
With such potent syllogisms 2325

That I've finally mastered it.
And minded once to marry,
I quickly found my wit
Was forced to yield up to truth
All its specious arguments; 2330
And I saw, like one awaking,
The dawning of intelligence,
Breaking through the covering clouds
Of ignorance and doubt.
And looking unemotionally
I see that Prince Bearne— 2335
POLILLA: *(Aside to Carlos)*
                              Look out!
More oil, the noose is tightening!
DIANA:
Is such a noble gentleman,
Worth all the praises I can give,
And far exceeds comparison. 2340
For breeding, there is not a soul
To equal him. For talent
He far surpasses any man,
However wise or gallant.
The very soul of chivalry, 2345
Submissive in obedience,
Generous in courtship,
And the king of compliments.
I'm so ashamed my ignorance
Has held me here so blind, 2350
I could not see what now I see—
He's really one of a kind!
CARLOS: *(Aside to Polilla)*
Moth, even if she's making this up
I swear to God it's killing me.
POLILLA: *(Aside to Carlos)*
Slap on the grease till it blackens your skin, 2355
Or upon my soul you'll never get free!
DIANA:
And so, dear Carlos, I've decided

To wed; but before I love,
Because you're such an expert, I wanted
To share with you what I'm thinking of.   2360
Doesn't it seem that Prince Bearne
Would be the perfect lord to give
Dominion over my loving heart?
Since I find him so superlative,
So far above the common herd   2365
That have paid court to me. What do
You think? You look so changed!
Has my idea astonished you?
(Aside)
Oh yes, he's good and wounded now,
I can see it in his look;   2370
His face has drained as white as a sheet.
I've accomplished all I undertook.

POLILLA: *(Aside to Carlos)*
Oh, sir—

CARLOS: *(Aside to Polilla)*
      I think I've lost my soul!

POLILLA: *(Aside to Carlos)*
Get a hold of yourself, you knucklehead!
She's got you stuck in her trap!   2375

DIANA:
You're not answering—is it something I said?
Why are you so upset?

CARLOS:
I'm surprised, to say the least.

DIANA:
      But why?

CARLOS:
Because it never occurred to me
That there could dwell beneath the sky   2380
A pair of creatures so alike,
So equally matched in size and weight,
Formed of such similar qualities
That none could differentiate.
And here I am and I see them both,   2385

And I can only guess we two
Were modeled on the selfsame form
So that I am a copy of you.
How long, may I ask, has it been, milady
That with such thoughts you've been so blest?   2390
DIANA:
For days this terrible battle has
Been raging in my breast,
And yesterday I gave up the fight.
CARLOS:
Why, that was the very moment that
I too made my decision   2395
To fall in love—it's tit for tat.
And just like you, my blindness was cured
By the sudden recognition of
The very beauty whom I adore—
I say, whom I desire to love.   2400
For certainly she merits it.
DIANA:
(I have him right where I wanted to.)
Then you were best to make it known;
Since I've kept nothing from you.
CARLOS:
Yes, milady, if only to boast
Of what a perfect choice I've made.   2405
The lady's Cintia.
DIANA:
                    Who? It's Cintia?
POLILLA: *(Aside)*
Bravo! A hit! He slid his blade
Along her edge and thrust it home
Like a champion. Very crafty, sir!   2410
CARLOS:
Don't you agree that I have done
An excellent job in choosing her?
I've found no greater loveliness
Or met with keener intelligence
In any woman I yet have seen.   2415

Such self-possession, such elegance,
Such kindness. Oh, I feel so lucky
In loving her. Just tell me if
You don't agree. Are you upset?
DIANA: *(Aside)*
I'm numb all over. I'm frozen stiff.   2420
CARLOS:
Have you nothing to say?
DIANA:

                   I'm simply stunned
To see you grow so blind.
I've never found in Cintia
The perfections that you seem to find.
Your passion's leading you astray;   2425
She neither kind nor beautiful
Nor smart.
CARLOS:
       It's unbelievable!
Even in this we're identical.
DIANA:
How so?
CARLOS:
         Just as Cintia's beauties
Are things you fail to see;   2430
So the excellencies of your Bearne
Are a mystery to me.
So once again, we're exactly the same;
We criticize with a single voice—
I, the man you've chosen to love,   2435
And you, the woman I've made my choice.
DIANA:
To each his own in matters of taste.
CARLOS: *(Aside to Polilla)*
This is going the wrong way.
POLILLA: *(Aside to Carlos)*
Don't panic now, the game's still young;
You'll get a chance to make your play.   2440

CARLOS:
Then, madam, if you will permit,
I'll leave you here to follow the sound
Of that enticing melody.
I'm so relieved now that I've found
I no longer have to hide how I feel;   2445
Since the reason why my heart now adores,
And the very moment it yielded to love,
I see are exactly the same as yours.

DIANA:
You're going to see her?

CARLOS:
             Yes, milady.

DIANA: *(Aside)*
Good heavens, what's to become of me!   2450

POLILLA: *(Aside to Carlos)*
Don't fold—she's got a losing hand.

CARLOS:
Farewell, milady.

DIANA:
           You don't have to be
In such a rush! How can a man
Let folly blind his common sense?
How can he let a stupid whim   2455
Overcome his intelligence?
What beauty is there in that girl,
What grace, what style, what simple art?
What has she ever said or thought
That led you to think that she was smart?   2460

POLILLA: *(Aside to Carlos)*
Raise the bet, sir, call her bluff,
And I promise you, sir, she's completely aced.
In spades.

CARLOS:
      So what are you saying then?

DIANA:
I'm saying that you've got terrible taste.

CARLOS:
Terrible taste? There Cintia is.   2465

Viewed even from a such a distance
You can see so clearly why
Her beauty conquers my resistance.
See upon that lovely head
Are woven tresses to ensnare,   2470
Oh, that I could be the victim,
Wound in the nets that trap me there.
Look upon that lovely forehead,
And below, those dazzling eyes,
There the sun draws all his lustre,   2475
And the moon, the stars, the skies.
Eyes that do not blind but bind me,
In such sweet captivity,
Eyes so black, and yet not slaves,
See, they make a slave of me.   2480
Look upon those blood red lips—
Coral is not more red—
Dyed with the sanguine color that flows
From the wound where I have bled.
See that neck of alabaster,   2485
Rising like a swan in flight,
Daring upwards to ascend
The heaven of her beauty bright.
Look upon that slender frame,
Would I could paint it, but I can not;   2490
There's an ethereal beauty there
More delicate than thought.
Lady, I was blind before,
And only now I see.
Where error made me a blindman once,   2495
Now love makes a madman of me;
I've haven't even given a thought
To how ungracious a thing it is
To sing another lady's praises
In front of you. All I ask is this: 2500
Give me your pardon and give me leave
To find out where your father might be,
And gain his consent to my wedding plans,

And to take the opportunity
To find Bearne as well and pay   2505
My compliments to your groom-to-be.
(And Carlos exits.)
DIANA:
What is this, my stubborn heart?
What is it called, does it have a name?
When a volcano erupts in your breast
And your soul's on fire? I'm all aflame!   2510
POLILLA: *(Aside)*
Heads up down there, here comes the fig!
Open your mouth and get under the tree!
DIANA:
Satin!
POLILLA:
   Yes, milady, here!
I can't believe the effrontery!
You didn't even defend yourself!   2515
Why didn't you lash out at this thank-
less fool, and leave nailtracks on his cheeks?
DIANA:
I can't think straight. My mind's a blank.
POLILLA:
What, did your nails forget how to scratch?
DIANA:
Satin, I'm burning up inside!   2520
POLILLA:
Maybe it's just your stomach growling.
DIANA:
I—the victim of his pride!
I—the object of his scorn!
This can't be me.
POLILLA:
   Be quiet, ma'am!
This looks a lot like love to me!   2525
DIANA:
How could it be love?
POLILLA:
   With a side of ham.

DIANA:
What's that?
POLILLA:

           I said it was love.
DIANA:

                     What's love?
POLILLA:
No, never mind, just the eggs plain.
DIANA:
I, in love?
POLILLA:

       How do you feel?
DIANA:
All feverish and racked with pain.   2530
I don't know what disease I've got.
POLILLA:
Give me your pulse and let me see.
DIANA:
Leave me alone—don't make me mad!
I feel such a rage come over me,
I don't even want to forgive myself.   2535
POLILLA:
Uh-oh madam, I swear to God
Your little veins are turning blue.
Not a good sign—very odd!
DIANA:
Then what's your diagnosis?
POLILLA:
You're having a bout of jealousy.   2540
DIANA:
You're crazy, what do you mean, you fool!
You clown, you boor, what audacity!
Get out of here. Get out of here now!
Me? Jealous? What are you talking about?
POLILLA:
But ma'am—

DIANA:

        And take your boldness with you! 2545
Before I have them hurl you out
The window!

POLILLA:

        Hey, look out below!
I'm going, madam, without delay!
You can't treat me like a chamberpot.
(Mother of God, she's so crude today! 2550
When a lady starts hanging out dirty linen
It's time to get Satin out of the way.)
(Polilla goes out.)

DIANA:

 My heart in flames? I can't believe it's true.
What can there be in a marble heart for fire
To feed on? In a breast of ice? Thou liar, 2555
Coward. Yet can I doubt what's clear to view?
 The only conquest I aspired to
Was over cold disdain. Yet higher and higher
He fans the flames of love. The gates of desire
Once opened, who knows what things may enter through? 2560
 I never saw the danger, I'm to blame.
I set a fire against my neighbor's walls
And saw the sparks from it set mine aflame.
Then wonder not, my soul, what thee befalls.
Since he who builds a bonfire in the street, 2565
Is usually the first to feel the heat.
(The Count of Bearne enters.)

BEARNE:

 I've won a major victory
If my good luck is true.
But there she it! Milady, you
See me before you at your knee 2570
Begging you to pardon me
For bursting in on you like this,
But I've just heard the news, which is
That I am yours—so small a thing,
But enough to send me reeling 2575

At the thought of this imagined bliss.
DIANA:
 I don't understand, are you talking to me?
What bliss do you mean?
BEARNE:

                Lady, I'll tell
You—I just met the Count of Urgel
Who said he was sure as he could be   2580
That I was to have the felicity
Of being yours.
DIANA:

            Well, it's not true,
And he's a fool for telling you,
And you're a bigger fool to trust
His word.
BEARNE:

       Though sense may doubt, we must   2585
Believe what faith compels us to.
 I know what a miracle it would be
If somehow I could get your love;
But it would be a denial of
Your godliness, for a man like me   2590
To reject that possibility.
This heart, that you are worshipped in,
Sees faith as its only chance to win.
The only way that you'll be mine
Is if my faith makes you divine.   2595
Goddess, forgive me, if this be a sin.
DIANA:
 But isn't it then a sin more base
To think yourself worthy of my love?
BEARNE:
No, because you're capable of
Making me worthy by your grace.   2600
And in this thought all hope I place:
Not trusting in my own desert,
But in the power you exert.

DIANA:

And he told you this fantasy?

BEARNE:

Yes, ma'am.

DIANA: *(Aside)*

      Of all he's done to me,   2605
This latest gives me the greatest hurt.
 It makes of me the discarded one,
Not worth his time, and him the great
And noble lover. He couldn't wait
To tell Bearne—he'd never have done   2610
A thing like that, there's no chance, none,
If he cared for me at all. The fight
Is done. Love, calm your rage, your might-
y hand has humbled my proud breast;
For there, the man has done his best   2615
And matched me spite for spite.

BEARNE:

 Lady, I've done this badly, I know;
The favor which you're showing me,
And the greater favor that's yet to be,
Requires a proper thanks. I'll go   2620
Correct my fault, and rightly show
Your father all the gratitude that's due
You both, and ask his blessing, too,
And thank him for the help he gave,
And for my happiness, and crave   2625
His pardon for having bothered you.
(Bearne exits.)

DIANA:

I'm all afire, I'm burning up!
What's going on inside of me?
If this is Love's revenge, then why
Should I wonder at his cruelty?   2630
It must be love, since his disdain
Holds my very soul in thrall.
His very coldness sets me ablaze,
And the little love-god conquers all,

Showing his power over my hard heart   2635
By melting it in his rays like snow.
What oh what alas can I do
To remedy this fatal blow
Which all in vain my breast resists?
Confession's my only remedy.
What am I saying? to speak aloud   2640
With my own lips my iniquity?
To say that I have fallen in love?
Here Cintia comes! My modesty
Preserve my reputation!   2645
And to the burning agony
I yet have suffered add one more,
The pain of suffering silently.
(Cintia and Laura enter.)
CINTIA:
Laura, I can't believe my joy.
LAURA:
Cintia, if it's in your hands,   2650
Hold on, who cares what you believe!
CINTIA:
Lady Diana, our kinship demands
That I show you the proper respect
As I have always done, and I
Can only hope that what my station   2655
Now requires, you'll not deny.
Carlos, Milady, has chosen me
To be his wife, and in him I gain
The fulfillment of my every desire
And the noble rank I would attain.   2660
Carlos is so in love with me,
He begs my hand, and I'm content
To give it, and all that's lacking now
To seal my joy is your consent.
DIANA: (Aside)
Love is just in his punishments!   2665
Over and over I feel his rod!
Have I not surrendered? What more

Do you want, you tyrant god?
CINTIA:
Lady, won't you answer me?
DIANA:
Cintia, I was marveling   2670
At Fortune—in what mysterious ways
She moves in everything.
Here an unhappy heart is yearning,
Full of doubt and anxiety,
Full of trembling and desire,   2675
For some good it cannot see;
And Fortune, seeing such sharp desire
Withholds that good, and then so cruelly
Puts it in the hands of one
Who never even sought it truly.   2680
I tried to make it up with Carlos,
Though wounded by his cold disdain,
Tried to oblige him with my favor,
But all my kindness was in vain.
All I got was scorn, while you   2685
Without asking, got his charms;
What he withheld from my desire,
He dropped unbidden in your arms.
I'm so hurt, I'm nearly blind,
And now you're asking me   2690
For my consent? I ask of you instead
That you avenge his discourtesy.
Let your scorn drive him to tears,
And let the burning shame
Of your rejection strike his cruel   2695
Heart, for mine is all aflame.
Exact my vengeance on his pride,
Meet his love with marble heart,
Let him cry, and sigh, and suffer
In your sharp disdain, and start   2700
To weep with—
CINTIA:
              Madam, what do you mean?

Carlos has ever been kind to me;
Why must I give a sharp rebuke
To one who's treated me graciously?
Why do you recommend to me   2705
What you yourself condemn? You tell
Me that disdain is bad in him;
Will it not be bad in me as well?
If he loves me, I'll love him back.
DIANA:
What is this love? And how can you dare   2710
Be loved by him and I despised?
Oh yes, you'll marry him, when there
Exists a heart within this breast
That's tearing itself to a thousand bits?
You enjoying his embraces   2715
While his spite, confounding its
Effects and causes, icily
Consumes my heart in burning fire?
First of all, may both your lives—
I swear by all the heavenly choir—   2720
Become the object of my revenge;
And with these hands of mine I swear
I'll rip him from my wounded heart,
Which he's invaded—I'll not forbear,
Though I must die with him,   2725
To kill his image planted there.
Carlos to marry with such as you,
When I am in such burning pain?
When his very coldness I adore,
And make a god of his disdain?   2730
But what am I saying, out alas!
To wound my reputation so!
They lie, my insolent traitorous lips!
They lie! But are they sinners? No.
While madness rages in my breast,   2735
How can my lips themselves restrain?
And yet by yielding to my grief,
I double the injury and the pain.

Death to the heart within my breast,
And long live my integrity   2740
And my restraint—Cintia, my dear,
If Carlos has chosen you to be
His wife, if Love to your neglect
Would give what to my care he denies,
Marry him then, and enjoy his love   2745
In sweet and holy marriage ties.
All I wished was to win him over,
Oh what a vain endeavor of
My haughtiness, for now I see
What madness it is to seek for love;   2750
Love is a gift that Fortune gives.
If one man is blest, another not,
It's always a matter of luck, you see—
What the poor one wanted the rich one got.
When a woman is loved by the man she wants,   2755
She doesn't *earn* the victory
It's all the influence of her stars.
If such a blessing never comes to me,
That doesn't mean that I don't have
In beauty and in reputation   2760
The kind of gifts that merit it,
Chance makes that determination.
Since I can't have the thing I want,
Since Fortune has my wish denied,
Take it yourself, she's favoring you,   2765
Give him your hand, and be his bride,
And may your heart find all its joy
In his fond embraces. Love can make
Marriage into—What am I saying?
And why am I driving a stake   2770
Into my own heart? I can't resist
What's happening to me.
My soul is going up in flames,
Good God, why should I try to be
Silent, when my eyes blaze forth   2775
The very fire I would disguise?

No, I can't resist it now.
While my lips are telling lies,
How can I hope to hide the flame
When the smoke is there for all to see?— 2780
Cintia, I'm on the verge of death,
My mad disdain has carried me
Up to this fatal precipice
By the path of my dishonesty;
And Love has punished my insolence 2785
Like an unforgiving deity.
Love is a child in all his games,
But a god in his vindictiveness.
I love! At last, I've said it now!
I love! and to thee I do confess, 2790
Whatever the harm it does my name,
Because my very happiness
You hold in your own hand.
Now that you've seen me in such distress,
Now that you've heard me tell you so, 2795
Wouldn't it be better to let him go?
(And Diana exits.)

LAURA:
God in Heaven, it's just like they cured
That crazy man—almost word for word!

CINTIA:
What do you mean?

LAURA:
                  Love was a dish
Diana refused to eat, till she heard 2800
She couldn't have it, then she gobbled it up—
And that's the thing that cured her spite!

CINTIA:
Oh, Laura, tell me, what should I do?

LAURA:
What should you do? You should hold on tight
To what you've got—don't let Bearne 2805
Slip out of your hands. Until you've heard
How it all comes out, hang on to him.

CINTIA:
Carlos is coming, mum's the word.
(Enter Carlos and Polilla.)
POLILLA:
A drop or two of the oil of neglect
Is a marvelous remedy.   2810
My prescription brought her back to life.
CARLOS:
If it's true, I've won a great victory!
POLILLA:
Put it on record, she's as good as cured—
She's already drooling over you.
CARLOS:
You know for sure that she's in love?   2815
POLILLA:
By Saint Peter and Saint Paul, too,
She's amorous! She's so in love
I had to run away from her,
For fear the poor girl'd risk it all
And tear *me* to pieces.
CINTIA:
                              Sir?   2820
CARLOS:
My lovely Cintia!
CINTIA:
                    Your happiness
Has achieved a triumph rather higher
Than that which rests within my hand.
Your insolence has lit a fire
To melt Diana's cold disdain,   2825
Which all the warmth and kindness of
So many princely suitors failed
To do. My Lord, you have her love.
And I resign my hopes, for her
And for you, if you want this victory.   2830
CARLOS:
Lady, what are you saying?

CINTIA:

That she unburdened her soul to me.

POLILLA:

All right, master, give it a shot!
There's nothing in the pharmacy
For ladies who are out of their minds   2835
Like a dose of incivility.
But look, here comes her father and
The princes with him. Get on the stick!
And no matter how sure of her you may be,
When you talk to him, be politic.   2840
(*The Count of Barcelona enters, with the Princes Bearne and Gastón.*)

COUNT:

My dear Bearne, you've given me such
Good news, I have to say yes. I'm very much
Obliged. And to repay, as is your due,
I'll give my daughter and my crown to you.

GASTÓN:

And, sir, though I have failed to attain   2845
The joy Bearne's been blest enough to gain,
I'll be content eternally
That he has won his victory,
Which I so longed to have—
Partly because of the help I gave.   2850
So to his triumph let me say "Well done."

CARLOS:

And to Gastón's good wishes, add another one.

BEARNE:

Carlos, I accept your congratulations,
And return to you my own felicitations.
In Cintia you have made so fair a catch,   2855
That I am almost envious of the match
Because it is not mine, but yours.
(*Diana enters behind a hanging.*)

DIANA: (*Aside*)

Oh what a mad impetuous course
My passion leads me on! Oh woe is me!
I'm dying of envy and of jealousy.   2860

All the princes are here together,
And with them is my father.
I'll watch them, but my heart's not in it.
And if I lose my joy, I'll die this minute,
And with me die my hopes.   2865
COUNT:
Carlos, you've asked me for my niece's hand,
And I, to satisfy your inclinations and
Your hopes, give my consent.
Our family's gain gives me such great content,
That yours and my Diana's wedding day   2870
May be the very same, I pray.
DIANA: *(Aside)*
And at the thought of that, I die.
POLILLA: *(Aside to Carlos)*
Diana's over there, sir, standing by,
Listening. You'll need to make a very clever
Speech if you want to get her. It's now or never.   2875
There are rules to this game of love you're playing in,
And if you miss this shot, you're not gonna win.
CARLOS:
My lord, I came to Barcelona,
Not to woo, but to entertain
Diana, and to celebrate   2880
Her beauty and her disdain.
And though it's true that I,
In the rosy brightness of
Cintia's beauty, have found
The dawning light of love,   2885
It was Diana's integrity—
So near my own, which forever
Gained such power over me,
Over my will, that I could never
Do a thing that displeases her.   2890
The high disdain that she has shown
I find so beautiful that I
Am bound to live for it alone.
And though I've pledged my love

To Cintia, my will defers
To what Diana's will might be,
For mine is only hers.

COUNT:
But who can doubt that she will be
Quite pleased with what you've said?

POLILLA:
Her Highness will say it herself, I swear,
Or may God have mercy on my head.
(Diana comes forward.)

DIANA:
I will indeed. But first of all,
Father, tell me, would you be
Content, if I should choose to wed
Any man from among these three?

COUNT:
Of course, they're alike in dignity.

DIANA: *(To the Suitors)*
And would it be discourteous
To you, if I choose him for myself?

BEARNE:
Your will is as a law to us.

GASTÓN:
Which all of us are bound to obey.

DIANA:
Then, gentlemen, it will have to be
That Prince who, though he pledged his hand
To my cousin, now should give it to me.
He who was wise enough to know
That only spite can conquer spite.

CARLOS:
And who is he?

DIANA:
                'Tis you alone.

CARLOS:
Then give me your arms, and your heart outright.

POLILLA:
And may my blessing fall on you

2895

2900

2905

2910

2915

Forever and forever, amen.
BEARNE:
And, Cintia, give me your hand.   2920
CINTIA:
I'm perfectly contented then.
LAURA:
And Satin, I'll have yours as well.
POLILLA:
I'm not Satin or linen or any kind of cloth;
Hold onto your hats, people, I confess!
Gotcha, Milady! I'm his man Moth!   2925
(Turning to the audience)
And so with that, and with your applause,
Our witty poet, most contrite,
Most humbly and most courteously begs
He now may end his *Spite for Spite*.

Notes to *Spite for Spite*

1–64 This section is in *redondillas* (see Appendix One for further details on versification).

3 *I've only just arrived today—* The text reads *por recién venido*, which may also mean "as if I had only just arrived'; if that is the meaning preferred, the line may be amended to "Pretend I just arrived today—"

13 *into such a stew* The text reads *tan mal guisado* (in such a bad way or mood).

18–20 *There's a lot more, etc.* Actually, what Carlos says literally is that his "indisposition" (*desazón*) has more "substance" (*naturaleza*) than Polilla supposes. It is not the weight of sadness, but despair.

22–23 *Remember what despair/Did to the Apostle with the bright red hair* One of the verbal cruxes of the play. Rico thinks it is the earlier allusion to "rein yourself in" (*te enfrenes*) that led commentators like Cortés to see an allusion here to the headstrong behavior of ginger-colored horses. Rico's own gloss is that the red-headedness (*bermejo*) more likely refers to the traditional color of the hair of Judas Iscariot, who hung himself out of desperation. Thus the Judas allusion begins a long series of jokes and puns on hanging. It reads rather like Shakespeare's early wordplay clowning (the Spanish term is *locura*, foolery); see for example either of the Dromios—but especially Syracuse—in *The Comedy of Errors*, or Speed and Launce in *The Two Gentlemen of Verona*.

26 *Are you at the end of your rope?* Some of the hanging and choking jokes and puns in this sequence are untranslatable, so I have had to find comparable allusions and fit them in where I could. This is an example of one such accommodation.

31 *I'm stringing you along* The Spanish proverb about giving someone rope (*darle soga*) does not mean the same as the English one. In English, it means to let someone get themselves deeper and deeper in trouble; in Spanish, it means to delay or procrastinate with someone to give them time to exhaust themselves in a fruitless activity—close to the English "give (cut) them some slack" or even the angling metaphor "give them some line (play)," which comes closest to the Spanish. I have chosen an English slang expression that seemed appropriate.

41 *Away with care!* One of those impossible-to-translate expressions lurks behind this phrase. The Spanish (*Polilla fuera!*) is a play on Moth's name, since the same word (*polilla*) means both "moth" and "care." (The closest we have in English is "butterflies in one's stomach" for nervousness or agitation.) In addition, at least in Lope de Vega—as Rico points out—*polilla del corazón* was a metaphor for jealousy. My "musty closet" is an attempt to capture some of that wordplay. The passage seems to suggest that Moth is prepared to do all the worrying for his master, and perhaps even remove its cause.

65–438 The first extended ballad passage begins here (*romance i-a*).

65 *Urgel* A town in the Lérida province in Spain, called in modern times Seo de Urgel (Martel & Alpern).

66 *Count Bearne and Count Fox* Bearne is the modern Berne, in Switzerland, at this time a French province; Fox is also a French province.

94–95 *public displays/Of skill, all to win her favor* Rico points out that this is one of two possible types of chivalric tournaments; in the other, each knight already has a lady whose honor and beauty he strives to champion in these various tests of arms and horsemanship and just plain extravagance.

195ff. *Her rooms she made, etc.* So Lady Diana attempts to recreate in her own quarters the mythical court of the chaste goddess Diana and her equally chaste nymphs.

203 *Daphne evading Apollo* Which she did, with Artemis's help, by being transformed into a laurel tree. See the song Diana's musicians sing (ll. 547–550).

204 *Anaxárte* This disdainful woman, to avoid her divine suitor, was turned, quite appropriately, to a statue.

206 *Arethusa* Diana turned Arethusa to a cloud to help her avoid the attentions of Alphaeus; but out of fear, she wept. Her weeping created a fountain, and the waters from that fountain were ultimately mingled with those of Alphaeus, the river god. (Rico)

213 *nor all his pleas* There are two readings in the Spanish behind this translation: one says Diana would not relent at her father's request (*ruego*); the other suggests she would not soften in spite of the danger (*riesgo*) to her father (of not having progeny to carry on the family name, presumably). My translation tries to straddle the two.

235–238 *Since one mistake, etc.* Literally, "since irrationality will all by itself lead one to error, and by doing so, will of necessity find itself overthrown."

356 *farewell the tranquil mind* The echo of *Othello* is deliberate in my translation; here is a parallel moment when the gallant warrior abandons all pretense of self-control, abandons his peace of mind and freedom (*la quietud/de mi libertad tranquila*) and commits himself to the potentially tragic pursuit of love-revenge (*esta furia vengativa de amor*). But what in *Othello* is serious, here is almost self-parody.

365 *What drives me now is more than desire, etc.* Moreto is very careful about assigning operations to the various sources of human activity, as those sources were identified in scholastic psychology. Much of the discussion—and the action—of the play depends upon a rather subtle and specific delineation of the various roles that affection, reason, and will play in controlling human action. This is the first instance in which that issue is raised. The key words in Spanish are *deseo*, *razón*, and *voluntad*, all of which terms appear in this passage in Spanish, and are direct translations of the equivalent Thomistic terms.

393 *It's natural, sir, etc.* This line does not appear in the Spanish, but is the gist of Moth's speech, and is presupposed by Carlos's response. See my note in Appendix Two about expanding or contracting certain speeches in the play for prosodic purposes.

423–425 *And he's not alone, etc.* I have expanded Moth's speech here from two lines to three, both to clarify the identities of Fox and Bearne, and to catch up prosodically after a slight condensation of Moth's speech about the fig.

437 *By singing the same sad song, etc.* What Moth actually says is 'by singing the Passion (*En cantar la Pasión*) on all the streets and streetcorners'. The Passion of Christ, was at that time, much like the spirituals and gospel music of today, a favorite theme of the blind singing beggars of the town. And even then, the Passion-songs had their erotic parallels in the plaintive love-songs of the age. (See Rico's note on page 82.)

439–546 This section in sestets, appropriate for serious matter delivered by speakers of high rank. There are irregularities in two places—in the form of short lines and alternate rhyme schemes— that have led some editors to call 439–516 a *silva*, and 517–546 true sestets. (Again, see Appendices One and Two.) My version regularizes them all to sestets.

471 *I'm a kind of reckless, wandering knight* In the Spanish "without this [amorous, courtly] obligation, only as an adventurer" (*sin ese empeño, solo aventurero*). Rico's note clarifies that Carlos presents himself as a kind of chivalric mercenary, crashing tournaments he was never invited to solely for the glory or the gain he might earn thereby.

494 *carrying plates* In the Spanish, the dishes are chicken, bread, and minced meat, and the costs of the various servings are to be borne the suitors.

540 *I could build a Trojan horse* Another verbal crux. The original edition reads *Seré Sinón, y ayuda* (I'll be a Sinon and help you). Subsequent editions read *Seré Simón*, etc., which most editors accept and gloss as Simon of Cyrene, who helped Jesus bear his cross. I favor Rico's reading, and his gloss of Sinon as the strategist who proposed and built the Trojan horse for the Greeks. It fits Polilla's profession of infiltrator much better. That Sinon was part of Renaissance mythology is

clear from Shakespeare's use of the allusion in Richard Gloucester's boast in *3 Henry VI*: "and, like a Sinon, take another Troy" (*3H6* 3.2.190).

542 *It's me sir, Moth, etc.* Literally, "Am I not Moth? Would you stop this? (Or perhaps, does this worry you?) I'll get myself into her skirts."

545–546 *Come on, etc.* Some editors give these lines to Polilla. Rico, I think correctly, assigns them to Carlos who says, in effect, if you can burrow in that far, I can get the rest of the way—into her heart (literally, into the vitals, *las entrañas*).

547–738 A passage of *redondillas*, with a few ballad quatrains for the songs.

547 *Daphne* See the note to line 203.

546ff *'Twixt love and gratitude* This verse initiates the major argument between Diana and Cintia, and is perhaps a little too hair-splitting for modern audiences. Cintia's argument in particular is subtle as only Scholastic arguments can be. Where Diana sees the danger inherent in any gracious response to a potential suitor, namely that it encourages him to continue his courtship and simultaneously compromises the lady who gives it, Cintia argues that gratitude is a form of justice—giving a person due recompense—and therefore proceeds from the reason; love proceeds from the will (583–590). Thus, she argues, it is psychologically possible—and therefore ethically permissible—to be gracious without committing one's affections or will. Indeed, it may be a noble obligation to be gracious (579–580). Diana responds that although this may be theoretically true (595–594), in the real world of chivalry and courtship, gratitude (esteem, respect) gives the wrong impression and leads men on, and leads the women themselves almost irresistibly to liking, and liking to loving. Thus even the harmless first step must be avoided, because of the danger of the final step. The argument takes an almost jesuitical turn when Cintia wonders whether the *potential* danger of love is worse than an *actual* breach of courtesy (612–614), to which Diana responds—in effect—that it would be, since the danger is mortal while the breach is only venial (615–616). Little wonder that such lines were written by a playwright in orders and only a few years from being ordained a priest.

649ff *Ego, etc.* Moth's responses are in Latin, and in bad Latin at that. Here, when asked who he is, he first declines the first person singular—incorrectly. He then identifies himself as "a scholar, poor and in love." His Latin in the original text apparently includes the accusative *scholasticum* instead of the correct nominative *scholasticus*. Rico's edition also reads *scholasticus*, though in a note he promises not to correct the deliberately wrong *scholasticum* of Moreto. So clearly something has happened in press, and the original *scholasticum* was intended to be retained. I have kept *scholasticus*, not out of any slavish fidelity to Rico's text, but for the rhyme.

654 *examinatus* What Moths says in the original to deflect Diana's criticism is *escarmentatus*—a completely made-up Latin word (based on the Spanish *escarmentar*) which we might translate as 'educated in the school of hard knocks'. I have chosen a more accessible Latin word for English-speaking audiences. It does not mean quite the same thing, and the jokes that follow are not literal translations of the Spanish jokes; but the idea is roughly the same, and the academic and medical imagery remains intact.

667 *In Acapulco* Moth concocts a ridiculous and impossible journey to amuse Diana and the ladies. I have used mostly Moreto's place names, though in line 668 I have substituted Viñaroz for the original Tortosa, for the sake of the rhyme.

697 *I could be a nurse* There's a hopelessly lost pun in the Spanish, since the word for doctor's aide or student nurse sounds like the Spanish word for "talker" with the connotation of "fast-talker"; so what Moth actually says is that he's such a "prattler" (*hablador*), that he could easily become a 'practitioner' (*platicante, practicante*).

701 *For the French disease, a silvery salve* The "French disease" is of course not only love but love's low effect, venereal disease—a common theme of joking among Renaissance stage clowns. The "silvery salve" (*unguento blanco*) is a mercury-based ointment used to cure syphilis. The Spanish contains one more pun; what Moth actually says is that he has just the medicine for the person

who is *franco* (meaning both generous, willing to pay, and infected with syphilis). Thus he is also begging for "remuneration"—to quote Costard in *Love's Labour's Lost*—a theme which continues into line 702.

704 *Averroës* Arab philosopher and physician (1129–1198), born in Córdoba (Martel and Alpern) and usually credited with re-introducing much of Aristotle back into western philosophy.

711–719 *Love, madam, is all confusion* The verbal echoes of Silvius from *As You Like It* (5.1.83–97) are intentional, as are the deflations created by the sudden drop into a comic closing line for the quatrains. This is done mostly to regain some texture for this speech, which is full of untranslatable puns in Spanish, all based on the word *quita* (to take away or deprive one of). Moth first says that love can "take away" reason, sleep, well-being, and ultimately hair (another venereal-disease joke). Women caught in love's snare always find themselves ending in *quita*—which is the Spanish affectionate and diminutive form—like Franciquita, Mariquita; and ultimately ending up *al quitar*—a legal and economic term which means "paid off once and for all by a single payment only"—what we might more rudely call a "one-night stand."

722 *Casabas* The original Spanish has the Toledo town of Añover, known for its annual melon crop, whose name permits a pun on *año-ver* (seen every year, thus annuals). I have chosen the more accessible (though imaginary) town of Casabas for the sake of English listeners.

727 *Satin* In Spanish Moth calls himself *Caniquí, cannequin* or thin cotton cloth (Martel and Alpern). Too many jokes depend upon the immediate recognition of this word to let it be the least obscure; so I have chosen "satin."

736–738 *now that his moth, etc.* Literally, "since she already has the moth introduced into her bosom"; again, the pun on the name, with something like the meaning of the English phrase "flea in one's ear" or "bug in one's ear."

739–1056 The rest of the act is in extended ballad form (*romance e-o*).

822 *a scientific mind* Literally, "a desire to know the origin or basis (of your opinion)."

861 *even when love was kind* In other words, much of the time Love kept lovers apart, but even on those rare occasions when Love brought them together, something else—fate, God—was sure to part them. This is reminiscent of the love-complaints of Hermia and Lysander in *A Midsummer Night's Dream* (1.1.132–155).

865ff *So then, since anyone who weds, etc.* Diana's argument is that marriage demands vows of love. So it should not be done *without* love because it can only end in tyranny; and it should not be done *with* love, since love can only bring tragedy. Therefore Diana has sworn never to marry.

945 *In practice as well as in theory* Literally, "without reasoning and argumentation (there) to support it."

977–979 *If heaven itself, etc.* This is a Renaissance commonplace, and also a Shakespearean conceit; see *As You Like It* (3.2.139–152).

996 *What a clean incision* Literally, "what a lovely cauterization!"

1028 *I'm a man of the cloth* Literally, "I'm the linen (she means)." The clerical pun in the translation—though not in the original—helps to prepare for Moth's transformation into Diana's "confessor" (2.1087–1088). So many puns have been lost in the translation, that I thought it permissible to add a few to help restore the balance.

1047 *You're leading her quite a merry dance* An English phrase, roughly, but not exactly, equivalent to the Spanish *Buena va la danza—con cascabeles* (The dance is going well—with bells on!). This saying also sits behind the closing lines of Act Two (ll. 1984–1985), where I have found it necessary to translate it differently.

1057–1304 *Redondillas.*

1064 *a couple of feet and both your ears* This joke is not in the Spanish.

1075–1076 *the surest straightest way, etc.* The wording of the Spanish is slightly different, but the meaning (they went the "wrong way") is the same. In the Spanish, Polilla says they took the straight road when they should have taken the crooked one to make her fall in love.

1080 *roundabout* Literally, "through the wheatfields" (*por esos trigos*).

1091–92 *Would you look, etc.* Literally, the Spanish says: "Look who she's entrusting her story to, so that it will go wrong." In other words the syntax is compressed for comic effect.

1097–1100 *Just like a kiss, etc.* The Spanish game is bowls, and the play is to knock your opponent's ball off the court with a glancing blow from your own (*golpe en bola*). So loosely, the Spanish says: "Be nice every once in a while to the poor guy, and, and like a *golpe in bola* when you've got him completely in love, you turn around and claim the victory." (The actual victory cry—*mamóla*—is colloquial, and much coarser than the English equivalent "gotcha!") Croquet is more familiar to an English-speaking audience, and the pun was fortuitous and helped me compensate for some later puns I lost (see note to ll. 1227–1228).

1118 *The lady'll bite, etc.* In Spanish, *Que se pique esta mujer; picar* means to stick or to prick (hence, *picador* in bullfighting); it's a colloquialism for falling in love, partially from the image of Cupid's arrow.

1127 *And what an unlucky day, etc.* There is a Spanish saying "to be in your thirteen," which means to be stubborn, unyielding; for us, the thirteenth day has other more immediate connotations, which I have chosen to use in the translation.

1136 *a lemonade* In the Spanish, *garapiña*, a shaved ice drink—perhaps, as today in parts of South America, a pineapple "icee." In America, a "slushy" or "slurpee."

1160 *partner for the pavan* The ceremony of colors was used to select partners for the *pavan,* a Spanish dance which is done with great seriousness, solemnity, and slowness, in which the movements are all quite deliberate. (Rico. p. 136)

1167 *Like a dose, etc.* Polilla's ironic comment is, more or less literally, "You're one lucky sick man; a cold drink is all it takes to cure you."

1188–1190 *So while I advise, etc.* Literally, "I intend to be a spy and a member of the Cabinet (at the same time)." Some editors think that the aside begins with these lines and not after them— in which case, Polilla would be talking to the audience about his intention to advise and spy on Diana. I have chosen to follow Rico here.

1204 *a very special slave* In Spanish, *el emplasto de ranas*: an ointment of mercuric oxide, used for treating venereal disease. (Rico, p. 139)

1212 *A double cross* Literally, "two games at once" (*dos juegos*).

1223–1224 *I could see that man at death's door, etc.* Some texts have Diana say she's incapable of being "conquered" (*vencer*); others that she wouldn't be "budged" (*mover*).

1227–1228 *She'll not only see your bet, etc.* In Spanish, the key terms are colloquialisms for kinds of bets in card games (*querer* and *envidar*) that allow for puns on love and hate (*envidiar*). I've chosen more familiar poker terms.

1231 *What a terrible time, etc.* The Spanish says: "It's a shame that she's taking (the) bull (now)." Much as this may sound like the common English expression, "to take the bull by the horns," it isn't. The "bull" in this Spanish saying is a papal bull, a document timed and promulgated to deal with existing ecclesiatical crisis or to grant a special license or dispensation. Roughly, the meaning is something like: "what an unfortunate time for her to make a stand."

1264 *Forget the sweets, etc.* Literally: "Rinse, but don't swallow." Proverbial: Don't swallow that bait. Moth's asides are meant to keep Carlos on track; every confrontation with Diana presents a real danger.

1268 *talking with tongue, etc.* Literally, "lying on both cheeks"—lying out of both sides of one's mouth.

1288 *horns* Horns of the cuckold, once a specific badge of infamy, but here—as elsewhere—a rather more generalized insult.

1305–1384 *Quintillas.*

1305ff. *To love, milady, etc.* Carlos's disquisition on love follows the Renaissance commonplace doctrine on what might be called the physiology of love (eyes, heart, imagination, desire, etc.).

Compare Shakespeare's "Tell me where is fancy bred" in *The Merchant of Venice* (3.2.63ff). Mixed with that is Aristotelian and Thomistic epistemology ("science of knowing") in a phrase such as "pass on...the images" (*trasladaron/las especies*). Rico's thorough notes on this passage (pp. 146–147) refer the reader to a number of sources, both theatrical and philosophical, for similar treatments of the same subject.

1347ff *Are they sorry*, etc. The text here reads *porque cansa su passión* (because their affection is tiresome); Rico amends to *porque causa su passión* (because their affection causes [discomfort?]; or, because it causes their [the beloved's] suffering). I've tried to straddle the two readings with my translation.

1360ff *But love is surely*, etc. The argument gets very refined here. Diana's point seems to be that the truest, deepest kind of love is the union of souls—in which case the joy of the union springs more from free will and rational choice than from physical desire. So "true love," being thus rooted in the higher powers of the soul, may reasonably expect a response from the beloved—at least a courteous one. (Is Diana arguing against her previous position? Of course; she's trying to get Carlos to respond.) But Carlos's answer is to catch her arguing against herself—then why have you previously argued so long and hard against lovers, if now you're taking the position that responding to love may be a rational duty? She tries to squirm out by saying that the response she means is one of courtesy, not love, and that she will act as she pleases. Carlos wonders on what basis she will make such decisions. When she replies that she will be the sole judge of what is right for her, Carlos answers that he is equally justified, then, in not responding; and the argument effectively stalemates. Part of the fun of this exchange is in the untranslatable puns in the Spanish since the same phrase (*tener razón*) means "to be right'" and "to have (a) reason" and the same verb (*querer*) means "to love" and "to want."

1385–1782 In the Spanish, this is in ballad rhyme (*romance e-a*) with insets of variant ballads (a-a and i-a) for the verses of the song. I have chosen to intensify the rhyming of this section (and elevate the diction) because of the dominance of music and ritual. Accordingly I have densely rhymed the introductory passage (1385–1398), used abab quatrains for both the songs and the speeches during the ceremony of colors (1399–1534), with one intervening couplet for humorous effect (1494–1495), and finally moved back into my normal abcb quatrains (1535–1782) for most of the rest of the passage. For further details and explanations, see Appendices One and Two.

1395–1398 *What's left of it*, etc. Taking a clue from the word *hartarse* (stuff oneself), I have somewhat enlarged the eating imagery of this passage. Eating is one of Polilla's favorite metaphors and I have lost some of the allusions elsewhere, so I have made it up a little here.

1418–1419 *his duty to show her love*, etc. The man's duty is to pay court to the woman; the woman's to receive his attentions graciously. Moth deliberately scrambles those duties later for comic effect (1474–1475).

1438ff. *Long live*, etc. This verse, like all the verses of the song which opens and closes the ceremony of the colors, is wonderfully sarcastic. I'm not sure if that's conventional, or Moreto's tweaking of the convention; I suspect the latter.

1473 *desert rose* Literally, "dried rose" (*rosa seca*).

1476ff. *The other way round*, etc. There are differences in the wording of Polilla's reply in the various texts, leading some editors to see a physical joke here (with stage business of Polilla turning around) and to insert an appropriate stage direction—similar to Malvolio's traditional "revolve" in *Twelfth Night* (2.5.139). Rico doesn't—so I follow him.

1480–1495 I have translated Polilla's speech a little more loosely than usual for the sake of comic effect. The original contains puns and colloquialisms that are devilishly hard to translate. For example, what I have called "two bars of soap" is in the original "two eyes of soap," meaning two washings. And the Adam and Eve allusion is not in the original, though the link between falling and sinning is. I've also rhymed it more thickly.

1528 *the ladies and gentlemen* Some texts read *galanes y danzas*—the gallants and the dances—instead of *galanes y damas*—the gentlemen and ladies.

1539 *upon compulsion* In the Spanish, Diana picks up on a word that Carlos had used in the speech defending his choice of mother-of-pearl, where he suggested that he was participating in this courtship ritual only under the force or compulsion (*violencia*) of his Carnival obligation. She suggests that his diffidence is a failure of nerve, but even more, of wit.

1593–1594 *Could a leopard, etc.* This proverb is not in the Spanish; Carlos simply asks whether it would be possible for him to change his nature. I've lost so many other proverbs in translation, that I tried to make up the difference by adding a few where I thought them appropriate.

1602–1605 *What are you saying, etc.* Diana is perhaps a little more coherent in the original, but not much.

1614–1616 *You wanted me to talk, etc.* The Spanish actually says something like: "would you prefer me to be such a dolt as would undertake to make something up, without making up some specifics?"

1642–1643 *Maintaining your integrity, etc.* In the Spanish, something like: "and in this way you have (simultaneously) complied with your own nature and completed the holiday obligation."

1708–1713 *make a plaster, etc.* As the reader may already have guessed, there's a probably gamey and untranslatable pun here. Rico calls the jest *merida* (rancid) as in meat gone bad. It's based on a double meaning of the phrase *traerte las piernas* (rub your legs). I've chosen the limbs/tree pun, which is certainly more modest than the original. Diana's "Ladies don't have legs, etc." is a fairly accurate but expanded rendering of the Spanish.

1743 *Gregorian chant* in the Spanish, the Passion (song). See the note to line 437.

1770ff. *Said Eve to Adam, etc.* This section is translated rather more freely than usual because some of the wordplays of the original are impossible to capture in English. For example, Polilla tells Diana to "make herself like Eve" (*ponte como una Eva*), an expression which can also mean to strip naked, "in order to make this Adam fall." The Garden of Eden allusions continue with a reference to her being the apple and carrying (or wearing) the snake. But the phrase "to give someone a snake" also meant to play a trick on someone. My version, while in places inaccurate to the letter, is faithful to the racy spirit.

1781–1782 *You say to yourself, etc.* In Spanish, Polilla says, "you try to take just one off the plate, and all the rest come tumbling after."

1783–1823 A miscellany (*silva*) in the original, with ballad rhymes (*romance é*) for the songs. I have stayed quite close to the Spanish rhyme scheme.

1793–1794 *The lady's tremendously light, etc.* The original has oxymorons: "See for yourself if this isn't a pretty hefty lightness, and a full blindness." I have tried to keep some of the flavor of those peculiarly Renaissance figures of speech (tremendous, light, see, stone, blind, look).

1803 *Shepherds in romance* Literally, "the shepherds of Arcadia."

1815 *medicine* In the Spanish, *polvos de Joanes* (Joan-powder), mercuric oxide. See the note to line 1203.

1822 *go to hell!* Literally, "go with Barrabas," the Jewish criminal whose release on Good Friday made Christ's cruxifixion an inevitability.

1823 s.d. *petticoats and camisoles* In Spanish, *guardpieses y justillos*. The women are definitely in *déshabillé*, though certainly not by modern standards. Perhaps they also have wraps on or available. The *guardapiés* is a long petticoat or hoopskirt, one of many worn under the overskirt; the *justillo* is a sleeveless fitted vestlike undergarment; 'camisole' is a nineteenth-century word, but seems to be the modern equivalent.

1824–1985 Ballad rhyme (*romance i-o*), with variant ballads (*romance é*) for the songs.

1915 *A cherrytree is a sight to see* Polilla actually quotes a Spanish proverb, which says, ironically, "How beautiful is the trunk of a cherrytree!"

1932 *Fenisa, wander, etc.* This line is of interest only because in the original text, Moreto apparently rhymes it with both the preceding and the succeeding line, a violation of ballad prosody. Accordingly, many editors amend it to eliminate the rhyme. Rico resists such emendation with the comment that Moreto is just careless here (*no demasiado cuidadoso*), as he is thought to be in much of his versification.

1959 *indifference* The Spanish word is *desvíos*, which means "wanderings, avoidances, aversions, insanities." Thus there is a particular appropriateness in Diana's word choice that cannot be captured in translation.

1965–1967 *I'm like a volcano, etc.* Literally, "I'm heaving like an Etna! What, I! despised and scorned! Polilla: That's right! Bless her soul, she might start hopping (*dé brincos* [boil over?])."

1984–1985 *Roll up the rugs, etc.* Polilla actually paraphrases two Spanish sayings here: "Governor, the dance is going great—with bells on"; and "Hopping like hailstones on a packsaddle." The first is easy: things are going just as we planned—and even better. The second is admittedly obscure; it suggests the opposite, that things have gotten out of control (as indeed they have for Diana). Hailstones hitting a packsaddle, because of the wind and the stiffness of the leather and the padding, are likely to hop about violently. The image, according to Rico, describes the extreme agitation of someone for whom things are not going well. (English has the phrase "hopping mad.") The "jumping, hopping, dancing" imagery is central to the humor of the moment and continues the earlier "heaving, bubbling, erupting" imagery of the volcano.

1986–2067 Tercets.

2024 *Till her pride, etc.* Literally, "until we've got her subdued by her own stubbornness."

2044–2048 *but she'll / Be forced, etc.* A complicated passage, rendered more or less literally thus: "She'll stand condemned as a fool all by herself; and when thinking is unsuccessful in convincing her she *ought* to love, in the suffering *that* causes, all our torments will be well revenged."

2060 *vengeance we shall wreck, etc.* Some texts read "your vengeance"; others "our vengeance."

2068–2198 Mostly redondillas, except for the songs, a supposed quote from Lope de Vega, and a *décima* supposedly of Bearne's.

2112–2116 A verse-form known as a *copla;* no one seems to know for sure if this is a real Lope citation; no one has located it, at least.

2123–2124 *if the pack of them spots us here, etc.* There's a card-playing pun buried in the original, which I have tried to retain. Polilla says, more or less literally, "if the pack (of them) sees us (together), we'll forfeit our ante." The word I have translated as "pack" is the same as the word for "game" in Spanish—*juego.*

2151 *some rather impressive verse* Literally, a grand *décima.*

2153–2162 The décima. Bearne's poem is one long wordplay on Cintia's name, which sounds like the Spanish words for ribbon, belt, sash, and perhaps leach (*cinta, cinto*), as well as the name of a famous Spanish actor (Cintor). Most of these are untranslatable. The fifth commandment — "Thou shalt not kill"—I did manage to preserve, as well as the final reference to the poem itself. In between, I have used other assonant English words that preserve not the sense of the original but the intention, and are kin to the love language of the other characters (sin, cinders, scintillation, rescind, sincere).

2171 *Oh, Geez* Literally, *¡Jesús!*

2172 *Pretty impressive, etc.* Literally, "That's something, (*mucha cosa*)—and yet my heart—."

2174 *Silence pu-leaze* An attempt to translate the extremely obscure and perhaps meaningless "Pus" of the original. Rico has a long note, detailing the many explanations editors have given for this monosyllable, at least one of which suggests it is a call for silence (p. 213).

2175–2178 *Who is Laura, etc.* Polilla's burlesque of these nameplaying love-poems is fairly accurately represented here, though I have altered the rendondilla rhyme scheme to doggerel, clarified the pun ('laurel/bay leaves'), and included a wink at Shakespeare (*2Gent* 4.2.38).

2195–2198 *I could go, etc.* The original is more than a little obscured by the wordplay on *poder* (could) and the niceties of protocol involved (who exactly "goes with" whom). What I have done is translate not so much the text as the clearest editorial gloss.

2199–2552 Ballad rhyme (*romance e-o*), and in a rare exception to Moreto's practice, the rhymes of the songs match the rhymes of the speeches.

2261 *Appropinquaccion, etc.* More dog-Latin, which would translate to "Approachment for speeching."

2262 *Mécum* Pronounced MAY-c'm, meaning "with me."

2274 *to Toledo from Madrid* Literally, "She's well past Illescas on the way to Toledo." Illescas was the final rest-stop before the last leg of a trip from Madrid to Toledo.

2283–2294 *Free will, etc.* More scholastic wrangling about human actions and their objects.

2298 *you're way in over your head* Literally, "You are ignorant of the argument"—in the philosophical sense.

2410 *Very crafty, sir* Literally, "This is black art" (*esa es doctrina del negro*). Rico glosses "black" in this sense as "clever, crafty, arcane." Perhaps it's an extension from "black" magic, or perhaps it's (not too subtle) racism.

2439 *Don't panic now, etc.* Literally, "Your turn is coming up, think nothing of this."

2451 *Don't fold, etc.* Literally, "in the long run, she's losing." I emphasize somewhat the card-playing imagery which dominates Polilla's running commentary.

2461 *Raise the bet, etc.* In the original Polilla uses the winning sequence of cardplays from the game of pintas—"five, six, and a match, total." I've tried to use a run of familiar English equivalents.

2469–2494 *See upon that lovely head, etc.* Carlos's description of his mock-beloved treads a thin line between real description and burlesque. The metaphors, of course, are all hackneyed; but even with hackneyed metaphors one can sometimes do wonders. Compare, for example, Shakespeare—whom I echo deliberately throughout—particularly Bassanio, in *The Merchant of Venice*, when some of the exact same figures are used to stunning effect: "The painter plays the spider and hath woven/A golden net t'enmesh the hearts of men/Faster than gnats in cobwebs." (*MV* 3.2.120–123)

2511–2512 *Heads up, etc.* Literally, "Look out, the fig has already fallen, and dropped by mistake into the mouth."

2526 *With a side of ham* This odd reply, literally "Could be bacon" is said by Rico to be—along with the later response "No, just eggs"—a traditional jesting answer to a foolish question. See his note on p. 232.

2540 *a bout of jealousy* Actually the word Polilla uses—*pujamiento*—which I have translated as "bout"—is more appropriate to describe a severe case of diarrhea or a bad spell of menstruation (Rico, p. 233); in other words, it's simultaneously coarse and clinical (which is typical of *gracioso* humor) and fuels Diana's outrage as much as the charge of jealousy itself. In addition, it initiates a series of scatalogical references that carry Polilla out of the room.

2547 *Hey, look out below* In Spanish, *Agua va!* the call to warn belowstanders that a chamberpot is about to be emptied.

2551 *When a lady starts hanging out dirty linen, etc.* I've used here an English saying that retains some of the meaning of the original. The Spanish is cruder; Polilla says something that sounds innocent enough, "when you start seeing shirttails, the cottoncloth is in danger." Actually it's not a shirttail, but a *pañal,* that part of the shirt that hangs down and is tucked between the legs; exposing it is a sign of great slovenliness and/or crudity (Rico, p. 234)—the equivalent, perhaps of going around unbuttoned, with one's underwear exposed. Polilla, being—under his assumed name—a kind of cloth used for underwear, jests that hanging around people with such an unsanitary attitude toward linen might not be good for him.

2553–2566 The original sonnet was Petrarchan; I have made it Shakespearean in the last six lines.

2567–2626 *Décimas.*

2582–2583 *Well, it's not true, etc.* Literally, "He's a fool for telling you something I don't even know myself."

2585ff. *Though sense may doubt* This fascinating exchange, in one way, is a mockery of the blind folly of such over-refined would-be amorists as Bearne. At the same time, it is, in places, a direct transference of Thomistic doctrines on Divine Faith and Justification onto erotic love. The first two lines could be a direct translation of a part of Aquinas's Corpus Christi hymn *Tantum Ergo: Praestet fides supplementum sensuum defectui* (Faith makes up for the deficiencies of the senses). Bearne's speeches make all the right theological points about faith, miracles, human unworthiness, divine power, sin, and grace that we might expect from a minor cleric and future priest like Moreto.

2627–2840 Ballad rhyme (*romance a-o*).

2670ff. Here begins the most astonishing set of speeches in the play. Diana's ultimate revelation, as much to herself as to anybody, of what's going on in her heart's core. For more, see the Introduction.

2794–2796 More or less literally, "Surely you can see, that now that I've put myself through the embarrassment of saying it, you'd better off giving it up."

2798 *That crazy man* The specific reference has never been identified, but from the context it is clear that the man in the story Laura refers to was cured of a phobia about something—probably food—by being forbidden to have it; after which he found it irresistible. See Rico's note on p. 243.

2814 *drooling* A typical reaction to the mercury treatment administered to syphilitic patients (Rico, p. 244).

2833 *give it a shot* Not exactly Polilla's actual image. The phrase *toma, si purga* (take it, it really works) refers to a laxative or purgative—a proverbial saying that is frequent in Moreto. (Rico, p. 246)

2838 *Get on the stick* Literally, "(speak) to the point." For anyone still in doubt about why I have used so many contemporary colloquialisms in Polilla's speech, I refer the reader to Appendix Two

2841–2877 A miscellany (*silva*).

2878–2929 Ballad rhyme (*romance é*).

2900–2901 *Her Highness, etc.* Martel and Alpern give this speech to Carlos instead of Polilla. I follow Rico.

2917 *and your heart outright* Not in the original, except in spirit.

2923 *I'm not Satin, etc.* Not in the original.

2925 *Gotcha* Once again, as in note 1097–1100, the Spanish victory cry *mamóla*, which translates literally as "sucked it," is equivalent to the English cry "'sucker!" of the ungracious winner. The extreme colloquialism of *mamóla* is followed by the archaic formality of *vuesa merced*, an extremely polite and old-fashioned form of address, which I have translated as "Milady." The juxtaposition is typical of Polilla's (and Moreto's) sense of humor.

2926 *your applause* Literally, "a winner" (*¡vítor!*), being the approving cheer of the Spanish audiences.

Appendix 1
Versification

Agustín Moreto's *El desdén, con el desdén* is written in rhyming verse (some more or less metrical, most purely syllabic), but not in a single verse form.[1] In the play, there are eight major stanzaic forms or rhyme schemes:

The *Couplet*, rhyming *aa, bb,* etc.,

The *Tercet*, rhyming *aba, bcb, cdc,* etc.,

The *Redondilla*, rhyming *abba,*

The *Quintilla*, rhyming *ababa, and* once *abaab,*

The *Sestet*, rhyming *ababcc;* and once (called *lira*) *abbacc,*

The *Décima*, rhyming *abbaaccddc;*

The *Sonnet*, in the Italian style, rhyming *abbaabba cdcdcd,* and

The *Ballad*, which is a vocalic rhyme rather than what English would consider a true rhyme. The Spanish ballad rhyme *(romance)* repeats the same one or two vowels (with a variety of consonants) at the end of each even-numbered line, for passages sometimes as long as four hundred lines.

The *Couplet* is a fairly unimportant form in Moreto's repertoire—quite unlike the powerful couplet of sixteenth and seventeenth century English drama. In *El desdén,* it is found only rarely, mostly in sections of the play (called *silvas* or miscellanies) where the verse structure is extremely loose.[2] Not all the lines in these sections are couplets—they really are little more than grab-bags of verse forms—and some of the lines do not rhyme at all. And those that do are occasionally of varying but unpredictable length.

The three-line *Tercet* is the equivalent of the Italian *terza rima.* Moreto uses a long line (at least eleven or twelve syllables) for his tercets, and uses this verse form only once—for 82 lines—over the course of the play (ll. 1986–2067).

The octosyllabic four-line *Redondilla* is one of Moreto's most frequent stanzas, as it is in much of Golden Age dramatic literature. It was the dominant form in the early Lope de Vega, but by the time of Moreto had lost some of its popularity. Throughout the canon, Moreto's use of the *redondilla* varies from 15–35% of the verse total, and in *El desdén* comprises about 20% of the lines.[3]

The *Quintilla* and the *Sextet* are two relatively infrequent verse forms, the second more formal than the first. The *Quintilla* uses five short lines, and the Sextet six long ones; and each appears only once in *El desdén*, over a stretch 80 and 108 lines respectively (ll. 1305–1384 and 439–546).

The Octosyllabic *Décima* is used twice in the play and is associated exclusively with the character of Bearne. In its first appearance, Polilla quotes a poem allegedly written by Bearne in honor of Cintia as part of his plot against Diana's disdain (ll. 2153–2162). Its second appearance is in the scene where Bearne throws himself at Diana's feet at receiving from Carlos the news that she has chosen to favor him with her hand (ll. 2567–2626). In both cases, this ten-line interlocking stanzaic form is just clever enough to be precious, and thus to mock Bearne's impossibly overrefined view of love and courtship.

The *Sonnet* form is used only once (ll. 2553–2566); and its sophistication follows immediately upon, and counterpoints, one of Polilla's cruder exits. Moreto uses this poem to initiate Diana's journey to self-knowledge, starting at the kind of reflective still-point with the sonnet, and leading up to the frenzy of the long ballad speech to Cintia later in the act.[4]

The *Ballad* rhyme (or *Romance*) is the most frequent of the verse forms in the play, and in Moreto generally, used here for almost two-thirds of the 2929 lines. It is in a sense roughly equivalent to blank verse, though it is shorter, is less metrical, and does have some repeated resonance at the line-ends. (Actual blank verse, by the way, is used only three times in this play—if those occurrences are not printing errors—and not very often in Moreto generally.) The *Romance* uses a loosely octosyllabic line, either masculine or feminine, with assonating vowels at the ends of the even numbered lines. This is an extremely flexible form, adaptable to conversation, low comedy, and high rhetoric alike. Its effect is often cumulative, as the form is open-ended; and part of the pleasure for the audience is wondering how long the poet will keep it going.

The Ballad rhyme is also used for all the four-line songs in the play, sometimes in octosyllables and sometimes in hexasyllables. As a rule, Moreto rarely uses more than a single quatrain of music at a time, and the rhyme scheme of the quatrain is almost never the same as the stanzaic form of the surrounding dialogue; even when both are in *romance,* the associating vowels differ. This is one of Moreto's idiosyncracies, which Morley notes as a way to identify his works and weed out spurious pieces. (164–164)

The following is the verse scheme of the original text. Notes to the text contain further information, including places where I have varied somewhat from Moreto's schemes. Not all critics agree about the names and the variations, so I have depended mostly upon Rico's analysis, with correction and corroboration from Kennedy and from Martel and Alpern.

ACT ONE

1–64	Redondillas	abba
65–438	Ballad Rhyme	(i-a)
439–546	Sextets	ababcc (439–456); abbacc (457–462); ababcc (463–546)
547–738	Redondillas	abba
	with Ballad Songs	(é) (547–550); (563–566); (643–646)
739–1056	Ballad Rhyme	(e-o)

ACT TWO

1057–1304	Redondillas	abba
1305–1384	Quintillas	ababa (1305–1329); abaab (1330–1334); ababa (1335–1384)
1385–1782	Ballad Rhyme	(e-a) (1385–1782)
	with Ballad Songs	(a-a) (1399–1043); (1420–1421); (1438–1442); (1530–1534)
	with Refrains	(i-a) (1453–1457); (1496–1500); (1517–1521)
1783–1827	Miscellany (Silva)	
	with Ballad Song	(é) (1798–1801); (1824–1827)
1828–1985	Ballad Rhyme	(i-o)
	with Ballad Song	(é) (1878–1881); (1892–1895)

ACT THREE

1986–2067	Tercets	aba-bcb-cdc, etc.
2068–2152	Redondillas	abba
	with Copla	aabba (2112–2115)
	and Ballad Song	(i-a) (2125–2128)
2153–2162	Décima	abbaa-cddcc

2163–2198	Redondillas	abba
	with Ballad Song	(i-a) (2167–2170)
2199–2552	Ballad Rhyme	(e-o)
2553–2566	Sonnet	abba-abba-cdc-dcd
2567–2626	Décimas	abbaa-cddcc
2627–2840	Ballad Rhyme	(e-o)
2841–2877	Miscellany (Silva)	
2878–2929	Ballad Rhyme	(é)

(Letters in parentheses are the assonating vowels of passages of Ballad Rhyme or Ballad Song. Letters outside parentheses are the rhyme schemes themselves.)

Notes

1. In his analysis of dramatic techniques during his own age, Lope de Vega made suggestions about the appropriate use of the common verse forms, but neither he nor any other playwright was slavish in following them:

   Acomode los versos con prudencia
   a los sujetos de que va tratando;
   las relaciones piden los romances,
   el soneto está bien en los que aguardan,
   las décimas son buenas para quejas.
   aunque in octavas lucen por extremo,
   son los tercetos para cosas graves,
   y para las de amor las redondillas.

   [So have a care to match the kind of verse
   To the subject that you're going to rehearse.
   Reporting news requires the ballad rhyme,
   The sonnet's good for someone passing time,
   The *décima* goes well with the lament,
   And octaves suit a grave predicament,
   The tercet's fine to deal with heavy cares,
   The *redondilla's* best for love affairs.
   (my translation)]

   Lope de Vega, *Arte nuevo* (1609), in Wilson and More (pp. 48–49). For a thorough and concise analysis, see Martel and Alpern (pp. xxv–xxix).

2. Morley identifies the four types of *silvas* that appear in Golden Age drama in general, and in Moreto in particular. In *El desdén*, the two *silvas* (ll. 1783–1823 and 2841–2877) are of the very loosest kind. See Morely (pp. 164–166).

3. Exact figures for this play and for the chart in the appendix are drawn from Castañeda (p. 28), from Rico (pp. 44–45), and from Martel and Alpern (p. 778).

4. Shakespeare uses the sonnet in his plays only infrequently, the best known instance being the sonnet shared between Romeo and Juliet at their first meeting. (*RJ* 1.5.95–108)

APPENDIX 2
Translator's Notes

From the beginning my intention as a translator has been to produce a script that would *play.* My work was originally commissioned by a producing professional theatre, The Old Globe Theatre of San Diego, California, known as much for its commercial success as for its commitment to the classics. So I would hardly describe my work as a typical scholarly translation. (So far as I know only two English translations even exist—both very loose and over a hundred years old.)

My fidelity has been more to the author's theatrical intentions—yes, I do believe such things exist and may be recovered—rather than to the letter of his text. Accordingly I have made some strong choices. I have translated into rhyming verse, because I feel that is one of the most important performance characteristics of his dramaturgy. Rather than laboriously transliterate and gloss the various puns in the play, I have chosen instead to try to find equivalent puns in English. The same is true for allusions, proverbs, jokes—in short for all the verbal currency that makes for living theatre and that needs immediate acceptance as legal tender by the audience if it is to pay off. And finally, I have translated Moreto's delightfully uncomplicated *siglo de oro* Spanish into what I take to be modern, often colloquial English, rather than attempt the kind of hopelessly *ersatz* seventeenth-century hybrid so popular with too many generations of Shakespeare imitators.

I feel an enormous obligation to do well by Moreto in this regard, because as he is virtually unknown in the English-speaking world, I would hate for my translation to introduce him to that world as anything but what I think he truly was for his audiences and still can be now—a witty, charming, skillful, and often extremely funny playwright, completely accessible at first hearing and free of the obfuscating dust of either time or pedantry.

Moreto is not a difficult playwright to understand; his passion for order and economy and his avoidance of artificial and overelaborate diction practically guarantee that. His vocabulary is not, like Shakespeare's, frequently archaic to modern ears. In all of *El desdén* there is hardly a single word that cannot be found in the most elementary of Spanish/ English dictionaries; even the clown's speeches are miraculously unencumbered by outdated or impossible slang. Connotations, to be sure, change, but even here there are few enough difficulties; and any major semantic differences are quickly clarified in the play itself by repetition and context.

The most likely obstacles to understanding occur in the more philosophical passages, where the conceptual substructure of Renaissance thought is exposed. Because fanatically Catholic Spain was more or less monolithic in its philosophy, the conceptual base, which it generally shared with the rest of Europe, tended to be narrower and more aggressively medieval—that is to say, essentially neo-Aristotelian and Thomistic. In a more Protestant and pluralistic society like England, the co-existence of competing philosophies and theologies muddied the linguistic waters considerably; and while the dawning Enlightenment brought about needed reforms in language, it also managed an almost wholesale redefinition of philosophical terminology, which further distances us from the philosophical discourse of seventeenth-century Spain.

So there are inevitably passages in *El desdén* which are difficult for English ears, essentially the debate passages; but fortunately, the obscurity is far from lethal, since neither side of the debate needs to be absolutely persuasive or even totally comprehensible. The supersubtlety of Diana's reasonings—she herself calls them "sophistical" at one point—is countered not only by Carlos's equally overstrained arguments (which we must remember he doesn't actually believe in) but also by the practical common sense of Cintia and Polilla. In other words, it is no great loss if the audience cannot follow every twist and turn of the argument, since it is to some extent Moreto's point that overprecision of thought (such as Diana's and to a lesser extent Bearne's) is self-defeating as well as self-deceiving.

The question of the unabashed modernity of this translation is a more complicated one. First of all, I can only repeat that this is a performance-oriented translation. Secondly, there are many things about

Moreto's style that make it amenable to a modern translation. He was himself a reformer of dramatic language, forgoing the excesses of Gongorism or even Calderonism in favor of a plainer, more straightforward style. His syntax is almost always simple, even colloquial; and his vocabulary, limited and familiar.

Still the question might be put—should Moreto be translated into something like late seventeenth-century English? Actually, thanks to the Augustan reforms of the seventeenth century, the English plain style of today—well, perhaps not today, but the day before yesterday—is not that different from the English plain style of Moreto's day. But the specifically *dramatic* language of late seventeenth-century England tended to be either bombastic (in the heroic plays) or mannered (in the comedies); only Dryden at times managed a simpler style on the stage, and even he only rarely. Further, poetry was reserved for serious plays, and prose for comedies; so there was simply no dramatic equivalent in England for what Moreto was doing in Spain. Thus, giving Moreto the style of any of his contemporaries on the English stage would be to seriously misrepresent him.

And inventing some kind of deliberately archaic stage dialect of English and imposing it on him would be even worse. And here we come to both a theoretical and practical *crux* of the art of translating classic plays. In a sense, a classic can exist simultaneously in three languages: the language in which it is written, the language in which it is performed, and the language in which it is heard. In Moreto's initial productions, all three languages were virtually the same. (Admittedly, his audiences did not speak poetry as a rule in their daily lives, but one must assume they comprehended it quickly enough in their theatres.)

In contemporary productions in Spain, some slippage inevitably occurs: Moreto's Castilian is not exactly the same as his audience's Castilian, and the performance language is probably a kind of compromise bridging the two. Modern performances in Latin America widen the gap even further; and either the performance language gravitates to the audience's dialect, so that Moreto is spoken with a distinctly Latin American accent; or the performance language remains staunchly Castilian, which has roughly the same effect as when North American audiences hear British actors (or American actors attempting British accents) perform the English classics; or the performance language is tugged in both directions and tries to straddle the widening chasm with a kind of neutral but "elevated" dialect, roughly equivalent to what is traditionally called (in Anglo-American theatre) Mid-Atlantic, or "stage speech." None of these solutions recovers completely the initial linguistic experience; all three are compromises. But the first two solutions attempt at least to draw two of the three languages closer together. The third solution, which has traditionally been viewed as the "correct" one, actually increases the separation among all three. (And then there is the potential "snob" factor in all this: that the "elevated" or "proper" dialect may be preferred by audiences, even when their own dialect might more nearly approximate what the original author spoke.)

Add a translator to the mix, and there is now no possibility of straddling. The performance language must favor the audience's language, or what would be the point? And there is even less of a point in attempting to start with the audience's language and then reeling it backwards in time to the approximate date of composition. In that case, the translator would be forced to write in a language which neither he nor any other living human being speaks with any fluency. What would be the point, indeed?

I feel very strongly that a translator must write—as far as possible—in his, and the audience's, native tongue. I think there should probably be no "standard" translation of a classic, though some (I keep thinking of Wilbur's masterful Molière) will have a level of artistry of their own that will guarantee them a longer life than others. I think, if possible, the translator should aim for a transparency of style and avoid calling attention to his own work by overcleverness or howling anachronisms; but that said, the translator cannot be so self-effacing or linguistically diffident that he does not know when to mine the potential of his own language in the service of the original. He must be in a real sense, as the actor must be, a collaborator with the playwright and not just an extremely clever parrot.

Translating Humor

In the matter of comedy, especially, a translator dare not be shy. All humor, from high wit to low comedy, depends upon correct preparation, efficient delivery, and quick apprehension. Nothing can be footnoted in performance, and jokes that need to be explained in a postmortem are already dead. When one of Moreto's characters tells a joke, the playwright has the clear intention of eliciting a laugh from his audience; and he will get that laugh if rhythms are right and the point is taken immediately. A translator who remains faithful to the text, but misses the jest, has betrayed the author's dramatic intentions in the service of his literary intentions—a fatal reversal of priorities, since the author's decision to write a play, rather than some nonperformance piece, clearly signals what *he* would consider primary.

Moreto's plays add another challenge for the translator as well in the person and function of the *gracioso*—in the case of *El desdén,* the wonderful Polilla. As I have noted above, Moreto's *graciosos* are, to a large extent, what he is famous for. And their specific linguistic habits—from the colloquial to the vulgar, and elevated only in parody—draw them closer than any other characters to the sensibility of the audience. The hearers become their sharers, their confidantes; and the *graciosos* become the audience's representatives and mouthpieces. More than any of the other characters, the *gracioso* must echo the speech of the onlookers. His proverbs must be their proverbs; his snatches of song, theirs; his jokes, their jokes; his tart observations, the very ones they would make if they had his wit.

The *gracioso* is not an outsider to the action of the play—certainly not in Moreto generally; but in *El desdén,* he is clearly a commentator, at times even a stage manager. He is, to say it again, the Spanish equivalent of the English Vice character. He simultaneously manipulates and mocks his betters. And it is almost always by means of parody, pun, and linguistic deflation that he achieves his comic effects. Accordingly, in translating Polilla (or Moth, as I have him called throughout the play), I have allowed myself even more latitude, permitting the occasional anachronism or colloquialism or modern slang to creep in where I have thought both the text and the context demanded it. His jokes and allusions are of necessity more loosely translated than the discourses and diatribes of his betters. And I have even permitted the occasional off-color remark or *double entendre* to stand—perhaps stronger in the English than in the original—because what was enough to startle the seventeenth-century Spanish audience may be too mild for the modern one and so, once again, miss the desired effect. A scurrility, like a joke, is there for the effect it has on the hearer; and it is the end which is primary, not the means. A literal translation that lacks the saltiness of the original must probably be deemed too bland for modern consumption.

In that regard, I have also given myself more latitude in translating Polilla's poetry into Moth's. In doing so, I have made use of prosodic strategies typical of English comic verse (many of them are the same in Spanish): burlesque of poetic forms; sudden injection of the vulgar or colloquial or homely into otherwise elevated diction; inappropriate metaphors; twisted proverbs; irreverent allusions, galloping meters; forced, inelegant, faulty, or over-ingenious rhyme. But even in the case of Moth, I have attempted to stay as close as possible to basic verse structure of the original. This, however needs some explaining.

What the structure of the original is I have explained earlier. The verse is almost completely rhymed, but in a wide variety of stanzas and meters. Since the *romance,* or ballad rhyme, predominates, let us start with that.

There is no perfect way in English to render the Spanish *romance* or ballad verse. I have generally used a very simple scheme of rhyming the second line with the fourth, the sixth with the eighth, and so forth—creating "ballad quatrains," in effect *(abcb)*—and only on a few occasions carrying the rhyme any further than just the two lines involved. The exceptions occur in three places: in climactic parts of the longer speeches where I felt continuing the rhyme further was useful or effective; at the ends of long speeches or sections or scenes for the same reason, where upon occasion I have used rhyming couplets in imitation of a similar practice in contemporaneous English theatres (but not in Moreto, generally); and in the "ceremony of the colors" (ll. 1399–1533) where I have opted for the more formal quatrains *(abab)* both in song and speech. On rare occasions this use of ballad quatrains (instead of the continuous *romance* assonance) has led to the expansion or contraction of a speech to place the rhyme more effectively for modern ears; but the slippage is never more than a line, and I make up the difference before launching into the more stanzaic sections.

As for the ballad meter, it is generally octosyllabic, with the normal occurrence of elision and contraction in the line as well as the occasional extra syllable at the end. I have chosen not to try to reproduce this syllabic line in English. Rather I have chosen to use a metrical, but not a syllabic form, with generally four (but sometimes three) stresses to each line and varying numbers of unstressed syllables. The number of unstressed syllables has depended upon the effect or the speed I wanted the line to have, as well as upon the need for extra syllables to make up the sense.

I have also made, when it was appropriate, a more generous use of the run-on line than Moreto does, partially because the true rhymes of English (as opposed to the assonant near-rhymes of Spanish) can get tedious without the occasional break afforded by hiding the rhyme, or gliding over it, by means of *enjambement*. In addition, because the ballad is continuous over sometimes hundreds of lines and because rhymed quatrains suggest a kind of closure, the run-on (especially at the ends of quatrains) helps to create a slightly stronger sense of continuousness.

Thus, for example, some lines from Carlos's opening monologue, written in *romance i-a*—so called because the assonating vowels of the even numbered lines are *i* followed by *a:*

> *La ocasión de verme entre ellos*
> *cuando al valor desafían*
> *en públicas competencias,*
> *con que el favor solicitan,*
> *ya que no pudo a mi amor,*
> *empeñó mi bizarría,*
> *ya en fiestas y ya en torneos*
> *y octras empresas debidas*
> *al culto de una deidad,*
> *a cuya soberanía*
> *—sin el empeño de amor—*
> *la obligación sacrifica.*
> (ll. 93–104)

And the translation in ballad quatrains:

> So there I was, among the others,
> Striving to prove myself braver
> Than my rivals, in public displays
> Of skill, all to win her favor.
> My valor accomplished what love couldn't do;
> I trotted out all my fanciest stuff,
> I went to the tournaments and the feasts,

If it was required, I did more than enough,
Whatever I could in the cult of that goddess
Whose worship exacted the ultimate price—
Not love of course, no trace of that—
But other than love, any sacrifice.
(ll. 93–104)

And later in the speech, for an example of the use of run-ons:

This was a haughtiness so cool
That any respect I had for her
Completely vanished out of sight.
This was too excessive to be
Simple composure, this went beyond
The boundaries of propriety,
This crossed the borders of mere reserve,
And arrived at sheer discourtesy.
A lady must walk a very fine line,
From which she must never waiver;
On the one side there's deliberate neglect
And on the other side, favor.
And etiquette requires of her
That she must carefully guide her foot
To touch neither one side nor the other.
If fondly she should slip and put
Her toe too far over the line
That marks the boundary of affection,
She cheapens herself. And if she veers
Too far in the opposite direction,
Trying too hard to avoid being gracious,
She ends up simply being rude.
(ll. 135–156)

The next most frequent verse form in the play is the *redondilla,* an octosyllabic quatrain with outside and inside rhymes *(abba).* I have kept that rhyme scheme in English, but again used flexible four- and three-stress lines in place of Moreto's syllabic ones. Thus, in the opening scene of the play:

CARLOS:
Yo he de perder el sentido
con tan estraña mujer.
POLILLA:
Dame tu pena a entender,
señor, por recién venido.
* Cuando te hallo in Barcelona*
lleno de applauso y honor,
donde tu heroico valor
todo su pueblo pregona
* cuando sobra a tus vitorias*
ser Carlos, conde de Urgel,
y en el mundo no hay papel
donde se escriban tus glorias....
(ll. 1–12)

CARLOS:
 I must be going completely mad;
The woman's spiteful—that's all I can say!
POLILLA:
I've only just arrived today—
Tell me the troubles that you've had.
 I find you in Barcelona; you're
A local hero. All the town
Praises your courage up and down
And your conquests. And what's more,
 You're Carlos, Count of Urgel by birth,
Which adds to your fame and glory;
If they ever tried to write your story,
There's not enough paper on earth.
(ll. 1–12)

For the tercets, the *quintillas,* the sestets, the *décimas,* and the *silvas,* I have similarly maintained the rhyme schemes, but used a flexible line, whose length mirrors to a certain extent the length of the original, but whose form is loosely metrical rather than syllabic. The one exception is the single sonnet in the play (ll. 2553–2566), where I have used a strictly metrical-syllabic Italian sonnet, with a slight different rhyme scheme in the sestet in order to end with the more familiar couplet to English ears.

More information about the original versification, and about my rendering of it, appears in the textual notes.

APPENDIX 3
Bibliography

HISTORICAL EDITIONS OF MORETO'S WORKS

Comedias nuevas escogidas de los mejores ingenios de España. Madrid, 1652–1704. A series of anthologies, published in forty-eight parts, containing some of Moreto's plays; normally referred to as the *Escogidas.*

Moreto, Agustín. *Primera parte de comedias de D. Agvstín Moreto y Cabana.* Madrid: Diego Diaz de la Carrera, 1654. First publication of *El desdén,* along with eleven other plays; seen into print by the author.

_____. *Comedias escogidas de Don Agustín Moreto y Cabaña.* Ed. Luis Fernandez-Guerra y Orbe. *Biblioteca de Autores Españoles,* XXXIX (Madrid: M. Rivadeneyra, 1856; reprinted, 1950). The standard edition of Moreto's works.

MODERN EDITIONS OF *EL DESDÉN CON EL DESDÉN*

Cortés, Narciso Alonso, ed. *Moreto: Teatro.* Madrid: Espasa-Calpe, 1955. Fourth edition of the 1919 original containing two annotated plays *(El lindo Don Diego* and *El desdén con el desdén)* and an introduction.

Hyde, G., tr. *Love's Victory, or The School for Pride.* London & Edinburgh: Hurst, 1825.

Jones, Willis Knapp, ed. *El desdén con el desdén.* New York: Holt, 1935. An edition for English readers, with notes, questions, and vocabulary.

Marston, J. Westland, tr. *Donna Diana.* In *The Dramatic and Poetical Works.* London: Chatto & Windus, 1876.

Martel, Jose, and Hymen Alpern. *Diez Comedias del Siglo de Oro.* 2nd Ed. Rev Leonard Mades. New York: Harper & Row, 1968. An anthology prepared for English readers, with introduction, glossary, and notes.

Rico, Francisco, ed. *El desdén, con el desdén, Las galeras de la honra, Los oficios.* Madrid: Editorial Castalia, 1971. A critical edition with notes and an introduction, which also includes two short pieces. Volume XXXIII of the *Clásicos Castalia* series.

Bauer, Roger. "Les Métamorphoses de Diane." *Wort und Text—Festschrift für Fritz Schalk* Frankfurt am Main: Vittorio Klostermann, 1963, pp. 294–314.

Casa, Frank P. *The Dramatic Craftsmanship of Moreto.* Cambridge: Harvard University Press, 1966.

Castañeda, James A. *Agustín Moreto.* New York: Twayne, 1974.

Harlan, Mabel. "The Relation of Moreto's *El desdén con el desdén* to Suggested Sources." *Indiana University Studies,* XI (1924), 1–109.

Kennedy, Ruth Lee. *The Dramatic Art of Moreto.* Northampton, Mass. *(Smith College Studies in Modern Languages,* Vol. XIII, Nos. 1–4 (October 1931–July 1932).

Morley, S. Griswold. "Studies in Spanish Dramatic Versification of the *Siglo de Oro:* Alarcón and Moreto." *University of California Publications in Modern Philogy,* VII (1918), 131–173.

Rennert, Hugo Albert. *The Spanish Stage in the Time of Lope de Vega.* New York: The Hispanic Society of America, 1909. Reprinted (without the appendix) New York: Dover, 1963.

Shergold, N.D. *A History of the Spanish Stage from Medieval Times until the End of the Seventeenth Century.* Oxford: The Clarendon Press, 1967.

Wardropper, Bruce W. "Moreto's *El desdén con el desdén:* The Comedia secularized." *Bulletin of Hispanic Studies,* XXXIV (1957), 1–9.

APPENDIX 4
The Francisco Nieva Version

In July 1991, The *Compañia Nacional del Teatro Clásico* staged a much acclaimed production of *El desdén, con el desdén* at the Festival de Almagro. The text used was a version prepared by Francisco Nieva, and later published (with a short introduction and extensive photographs) by the Ministry of Culture in 1991 as part of its classical theatre collection. The published text was the basis of the production, although a note on the copyright page warns the reader that it does not necessarily include every modification that may have been made in the rehearsal and performance process.

In Appendix Two, I noted that preparing classical texts for modern audiences presented difficulties and challenges even apart from language-to-language translation. There are other kinds of translations as well, even within the same language: the translation from one linguistic period to another (comparable in a way to bringing the early modern English of Shakespeare to late modern ears), the translation from one stage of a culture to another (from a Renaissance or *siglo de oro* worldview to a modern or even post-modern sensitivity), and more specifically from one set of audience expectations to another.[1] The Nieva text provides a kind of testcase.

The first things one notes about the Nieva text is that it is some 471 lines shorter and is divided into two acts instead of the classical three.

Thus, almost one-sixth of the play's 2929 lines have been cut—which is in my experience fairly typical of the way that directors and dramaturges deal with presenting longish classical texts to modern audiences with notoriously short attention spans. (Typically, Shakespeare plays of 2500–3500 lines are cut by anywhere from 1/3 to 1/6 to ensure the fairly standard 2 1/2 to 2 3/4 hour total running time expected by modern theatre-goers. At 15 lines per minute, a 3000-line play would run 200 minutes—that's three hours and ten minutes, *excluding* intermissions. A 2000-line cutting of the same play would run 133 minutes, or two hours and thirteen minutes, permitting a single seventeen-minute intermission.) Moreto's line are generally shorter than the typical Shakespearean pentameters, so I estimate that the 2458 lines of the Nieva version (at 17 *lpm*) would run just under two and half hours, close enough—with only one intermission, which Nieva supplies just before the Garden scene (between the original lines 1782 and 1783)—to suit the modern audience. (The single intermission is the overwhelming choice of modern Shakespeare directors as well.)

Actually, Nieva cuts a few more than 471 lines, closer to 485—it is hard to be exact because there is substantial rewriting in addition to the cutting. He *adds* lines at the end to pair up the couples more formally (which Moreto did only peremptorily), to clarify a joke or two, and occasionally to supply what are known as "blends" to smooth over gaps between lines on either side of a cut. (All of these are again fairly typical of modern Shakespearean practice.)

It is not so much *that* he cuts, but *what* he cuts, that is important. The major cuts occur in four scenes: Carlos's long expository narrative (65–393); the first interview between the princes and Diana (813–960); Carlos's and Diana's encounter after the ceremony of the colors (1535–1696); and the plots of the princes and Carlos at the opening of Act Three (1986–2124). Cuts in the first section total 210 lines; in the second, 35 lines; in the third, 48 lines; and in the fourth, 64 lines; so the three sections account for 357 line cuts or three-fourths of the total.

Clearly one principle of Nieva's cutting is to excise portions of the script that are more rhetorical or analytical than strictly dramatic. Carlos's opening monologue is a typical Moretan device; and for all its virtuosity, Nieva clearly sees it as almost more of a challenge for the audience who must hear it, than for the actor who must speak it. The monologue is not action, but exposition; Carlos's psychological journey is recounted rather than shown; it is, in Nieva's opinion, non-dramatic and disposable. The debate between Diana and the princes is, likewise, non-dramatic and analytical; and the debate between Diana and Carlos in the third section is heavily philosophical; both can be trimmed. Finally, the plotting that opens Act Three needs only the barest outline to make its point. Its purpose is to set up the comedy of the final act; too much analysis slows down the action, especially at this critical moment when the audience senses the end is near.

It might well be objected that what Nieva finally accomplishes with cuts like this is a partial deMoretification of the text. The long expository monologue, the subtlety of philosophical debate, and the depth of psychological analyses—these are hallmarks of Moreto's style, all of which fall victim to Nieva's knife. And to a certain extent, the charge must be admitted. Language is ever the sacrificial lamb to the cry for action on the stage—ancient as well as modern. And the undeniable de-verbalizing effects of film and television in the twentieth century have only aggravated the problem.

The remaining cuts in the script fall into a number of fairly obvious categories: subtleties of seventeenth century thought or manners, textual obscurities, learned allusions, jokes that don't work—these are sometimes simply cut, or quite frequently re-written. And rewriting is something that Nieva does almost continuously: word substitution—familiar for the unfamiliar; word order or syntactical re-alignment—modern for archaic or difficult; slight changes of meaning more easily or immediately grasped by modern audiences; clarifying of obscurities of language or allusion or humor. There is scarcely a page without a substantial number of such changes.

In the first thirty lines alone, for example, where there are no cuts, there are variations from the standard text—of one kind or another, excluding the merely orthographical—in nine of the lines. The more complex the verse form, the more intricate the rhyme scheme, the harder it is to make changes; as a result the majority of cuts and rewrites are in the ballad rhyme sections.

And this brings us to a further observation—that although Nieva's general practice is to retain the rhyme scheme amidst all his cuts and rewrites, in at least two instances—once in a tightly rhymed section and once in a loosely rhymed section—he makes changes that violate the essential verse form of the original. (This is a fault, I think, but not unknown in Shakespeare cutting, where one often finds the meter or the line length scrambled by modern cutting or rewriting. But the fault is more glaring in Moreto than in Shakespeare because of the rigidity of Moreto's forms and the flexibility of Shakespeare's, along with the latter's more than occasional looseness in handling them.)

Overall I would estimate the number of Nieva's rewrites to total at least 25% of the lines left uncut. So if one-sixth of the play has been cut, and one-fourth of the remaining lines have been rewritten, we must say that Nieva, even in preparing a Spanish-language version, has made substantial changes in the text to bring it from the *siglo de oro* to the late twentieth century. And we have to grant further that some of the specifically Moretan qualities of the original (which I identify in the Introduction) have clearly been "lost in translation."

Note

1. There is a burgeoning critical interest in the phenomenon of cross-cultural translation of the theatrical classics, but as yet even the preliminary data-gathering phase is only barely underway. While an enormous amount of theoretical work has been done recently on the classics, literary as well as theatrical, with an eye to identifying the exact relationship (or "encounter" as it is sometimes called) between the modern *reader* and the classical *text,* next to nothing has been done on the specific subject of the modern director, actor, and audience and the classical *playscript.* Most of what exists is confined to the chatty interview, the occasional review, the passing comment, the colorful anecdote, the casual table-talk, the self-serving program note, and (most often) the faulty and half-hearted extension of "reading" theory to the far more complex phenomenon of the stage. Roger Gross's *Understanding Playscripts* (Bowling Green, 1974) is a happy exception. More typical are the perceptive comments of Charles R. Lyons in his Introduction to *Critical Essays on Henrik Ibsen* (Boston, 1987), who pinpoints the problem (in passing) without providing a comprehensive overview or suggesting a possible solution:

> The radical difference between the activities of reading a text and experiencing a play in performance has always complicated the project of dramatic criticism. Even the most sophisticated and skillful of analysts have vacillated among various rhetorical strategies that do not always clarify whether they consider the dramatic text as a literary work equivalent to poetry or fiction, as the score for a hypothetical performance, or as a written document that has been subject to a history of theatrial production and is encumbered with unofficial appendices of critical glosses and established conventions of performance. While the idea of performance persistently intervenes in the critical project, commentators rarely define the nature and function of that performance precisely. (3–4)

DAKIN MATTHEWS is an actor, director, playwright, dramaturge, teacher, and Shakespeare scholar. He is currently the Manager of the Antaeus Company at the Mark Taper Forum and a Dramaturge for the Old Globe Theatre in San Diego. For five years he was the Artistic Director of the Berkeley Shakespeare Festival, and before that of the California Actors Theatre. He is an Emeritus Professor of English at California State University Hayward and has been a busy stage and screen actor for almost thirty years, in over 150 professional plays, thirty feature films, TV movies, and miniseries, and has appeared in more than one hundred television shows. He is a member of both the Motion Picture and the Television Academy. He has acted, taught, and directed in major theatres and training schools across the country, including Juilliard, the Old Globe, the Acting Company, and ACT in San Francisco. His scripts—adaptations, translations, and originals—have been performed at Juilliard, the Goodman Theatre, the Old Globe, California Actors Theatre, California and Berkeley Shakespeare Festivals, and the American Conservatory Theatre.